7.5 Secrets To A Successful Blog

Lon Safko
www.LonSafko.com

Dr. Gary A. Witt
www.marketingpsychology.com

Dr. Gary A. Witt
www.marketingpsychology.com

Lon Safko
www.LonSafko.com

Copyright © 2016, Dr. Gary A. Witt, & Lon Safko.

Created in the United States of America.

ISBN-13: 978-1535183833

ISBN-10: 1535183837

What The Experts Are Saying About
7.5 Secrets To A Successful Blog

What The Experts Are Saying About
7.5 Secrets To A Successful Blog

"Blogs are free like a puppy, not free like a beer. This book provides new and proven methods to ensure your hard work turns into readers."
Erik Qualman, Author of Socialnomics

"Wow. This is a goldmine. Seriously, there's a year's worth of insight and information in this e-book. Lon Safko and Dr. Gary Witt have done a fabulous job and have provided some amazing insights to boot — brilliant!"
Jamie Turner, Internationally-Recognized Author, Speaker and CEO of 60 Second Marketer and 60 Second Communications "

This book has incredibly valuable analysis of what a successful blog post looks like. You can easily see what words and images work and which ones don't. Keep this handy for the next time you want to knock it out of the park with a post that will get shared and read.

Love it!"
Andrea Vahl, Co-author of Facebook Marketing All-in-One for Dummies

"This eBook should be disseminated liberally with the content marketers on your team AND be printed out and left on your desk for easy access and reference! Not only have Lon and Gary created an essential resource for every blogger out there, but they have done so by tapping into the works of one of the most successful content marketers in the world (and all around likeable guy) Dave Kerpen. This isn't some wishy washy fluff piece! "7.5 secrets to a Successful Blog" gives you truly actionable advice and strategies. I'll be referring it to my clients who want to amp up their game blogging on LinkedIn Publisher!"
Viveka von Rosen, Author of LinkedIn Marketing: An Hour a Day

"This is an enjoyable deep dive into the analytics of one of the rock stars in my industry - Dave Kerpen. Dr. Witt, and Lon Safko, being the scientists they are, decided there had to be a "Law of Nature" that determines success. Good for them to look deeply into this. The Take-aways are totally doable and being put into play right now in my marketing. Highly recommended."
Phyllis Khare, Co-Founder of Social Media Manager School and Founder of TimeBliss.ME

"I wish I could have had this book years ago. In here are the answers to the questions we ask every time we start a blog post, answers that are backed by research. More than any treatise on blogging I've seen, 7.5 Secrets uses real research and psychology to identify ways to turn our blogs into business-builders. I expect this book to be instrumental in growing my blog traffic, subscriber list and new website optimization clients by an order of magnitude."
Brian Massey, The Conversion Scientist

"Grab yourself a coffee, and this book! It is a stats-backed, fact-packed overview of what is making Dave's content fly. Lon and Gary did a fantastic job of pulling out the most important factors, one by one. New blogger? Your eyes will be opened to the art and science behind this, and if you are a veteran blogger you will freshen your view, given you new insight and inspiration. P.S. keep a pen and paper handy - make notes, it will be worth it!"
Martin Shervington, Founder & Community Manager at PlusYourBusiness.com, Inc. The Academy

"Not only does this book show how to create a successful blog, it even drills down to headline strategies, best words to use and how to select picture. This takes the art of a blog to a whole new level."
Chuck Martin, NY Times Business Bestselling Author

Table of Contents

Chapter 1

Introduction

Chapter 1 Introduction

You write your blog, upload it with hope, and nothing, a few dozen people view it! What a waste of your time and creativity. How did you fail? **This book will reveal new, proven ways you can get more readers, not just for your blogs, but for your e-mails, brochures, advertisements, and other marketing materials as well.**

The gatekeeper in any blog's success is the TITLE. Fail with that and nothing else matters. It is the same with any print advertising and direct mail marketing. The Niagara torrent of information unleashed by the Internet has changed the way we interact with information. People scan today, giving you 1.5 seconds (more on that later), to grab their attention before they are gone. Your title must immediately seduce them and make them want more.

That is true not only with titles, but content as well. You must adjust your style, words, and layout to the *New Normal* of reading to keep people after they open your blog or e-mail. In this book you'll learn some surefire style and content methods to hold your readers. People have changed. And, so must writers. Here is how to do it.

How This Book Will Help You:

You will learn:
- ✓ 63 powerful ways to craft a title people will want to open, read, like, and share.
- ✓ 19 surprising mistakes in titles and pictures you must avoid.
- ✓ Golden words in your title that boost readership.
- ✓ How to design your blog's layout to satisfy readers' New Normal expectations.
- ✓ Proven lessons from advertising and direct mail research to grab readers and keep them.

What's Inside
- ✓ Analysis of 22 common words, phrases and symbols, rated from 1 to 5 Stars.
- ✓ Analysis of types of promises made by your title.
- ✓ Analysis of the power of odd vs. even numbers and the length of your title.
- ✓ Analysis of 'hot words' used alone and in groups that bring in readers.
- ✓ How to put these lessons into practice.
- ✓ Detailed findings in table form for deeper study and insights.
- ✓ Videos by Dr. Witt and Mr. Safko to help you understand these ideas in more detail.
- ✓ Visual presentation to clarify ideas and let you help others learn.

Who We Are

Dr. Gary Witt is an expert on buyer behavior with a Ph.D. from the University of Texas in both psychology and communication. After two decades in marketing for corporations, associations and political candidates, he now is a professor of marketing, psychology and communication at five Universities. He authored both a university textbook and an advertising psychology book, *High Impact: How To Create Ads That Sell!* See full bio in Appendix.
http://www.MarketingPsychology.com

Lon Safko is the author of two best-selling business books, *The Social Media Bible*, and *The Fusion Marketing Bible*. He is a popular international corporate speaker on social media, fusion marketing and other advanced marketing techniques, winner of Inc. Magazine's Entrepreneur of the Year, and a highly successful blogger. See full bio in Appendix.
http://www.LonSafko.com

Dave Kerpen, on whose data this book is based, had 16,000,000 readers of his LinkedIn blogs in 2013, including one blog with 2.7 million readers! Without this data on Dave's 132 blogs, the insights you will discover would not have been possible. See Dave's own take on his success in his article written for INC Magazine "How to Make Money by Blogging on LinkedIn." http://bit.ly/1ykZGiB.See full bio in Appendix.
http://www.likeable.com/

How This Book Happened

Lon writes, a good friend of mine is a prolific content generator, author of NYT bestselling books, blogs, articles, tweets, status updates, and posts. His name is Dave Kerpen. He is the author of the phenomenally successful book *Likeable Social Media* and has built an agency around it. Dave is the most read LinkedIn blogger to date with more than 2,000,000 Views with just one of his blogs! Dave and I met due to our common achievements of both having bestselling books in the social media industry.

I shared with Dave an insight or two into what has been working in my blogs and what hasn't. He shared his own analysis of the success of his blog posts.

Dave says your headline is the single most important factor in success and must deliver a succinct promise, as others have said. Next up in importance is the hero image at the top of the post, followed (last) by the content itself. The number one factor in determining virility is rate of comments, so best to solicit comments in both the post and offline amongst friends. Publishing time is also important. He says that Monday thru Wednesday in the morning is the best time to post, although this varies more now with so many others publishing.

All that said, Dave has had posts that have had as few as 2K Views and posts with as many as 2M Views; so obviously there are other factors including luck at play

Here are Dave's six steps to a successful blog:

1. Think of a great headline.
2. Use a compelling photo.
3. Write a concise post.

4. Include two strong "calls to action" at the bottom of your post.
5. Share the post on LinkedIn, Facebook and Twitter.
6. Repeat steps 1 through 5 in all your future blogs.

How You Can Get the Most Out of This Book

You can benefit from what follows in two ways – one is a "quickie," and the other is deeper. We believe this will be the **New Normal for e-books**, with basic information presented in a skimable format for easy digestion, and more detailed information linked to it for those who want to know more. Like looking at an iceberg, the Quickie Approach shows you the top, while the Deeper approach gives you a more in-depth look at the topic, with fast access back and forth.

Quickie Approach: A quick way to get the basic findings. You can apply the specific ideas you find here to each of your new blog titles. Insights like words to use and to avoid, symbols to stay clear of, pictures that help, how to

7

couch your WIIFM (What's In It For Me?) pitch, and so on.

Deeper Approach: Don't just settle for the "How;" also understand the "Why." Why did these techniques create hundreds of thousands of Views for Dave's blogs? Why do readers make the choices they do? Learn this and all your writing will improve. You'll better understand Dr. Witt's principles of Marketing Psychology which govern how buyers make decisions and are at the root of all analysis in this book. You'll find explanations throughout the book in the Deeper Approach by clicking "Read More" in the Quickie paragraphs. The return link pops you back to where you were.

Note: To maintain the "Quickie" / "Deeper" format of this book, you will find analysis tables in the appendix, which can be accessed through the anchor links.

As you move through the book, you'll find each of the 7.5 promised secrets shown in red so you don't miss them. Each one is rooted in the findings, but offers you a broader view on blogging based on our research. We hope you find them helpful in creating your own popular blogs!

Chapter 2

Data & Methods

Russell Crowe as Professors John Nash in "A
Beautiful Mind"

Statistics and data are often boring, so you may be inclined
to skip this chapter. That's fine. Those who want to
understand the foundation for our analysis should read it.

We analyzed a total of 132 blogs. While several of Dave's
blogs were over 2,000 words, most settled in at about 900
words. The number of blog Views ranged from 2,655 to
over 2 million! The full data is proprietary and is not made
available here.

	Views	Likes	Comments
Lowest readership blog	2,655	36	10
Highest readership blog	2,718,988	26,898	7,499

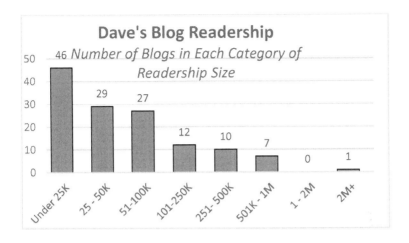

Blog Views by size categories (Chart Table).

0k<25k	46
25k<50k	29
51k<100k	27
101k<250k	12
251k<500k	10
501k<1m	7
1m<2m	0
2m+	1
Total	**132**

Categories of Data

We compared the best and worst performing titles to find differences that made the best titles stand out. We looked at two categories: the top and bottom 25% and 33% of titles by the number of Views they had. Here is the breakdown:

- Bottom 25%: 33 titles. Below 18,000 Views.
- Bottom 33%: 44 titles. Below 24,500 Views
- Top 33%: 44 titles. Above 57,000 Views

11

- Top 25%:   33 titles. Above 74,500 Views.

The median number of Views for Dave's blogs was 41,191, still a Wow! number of readers.

A Quick Disclaimer You Need To Read

In statistical research a number like 132 is not many. A rule of thumb is that you need over 350 subjects to get results at the 95% confidence level. (It's more complex than that, but this makes my point). Since we broke down blog titles in many different ways, those subgroups usually had few examples. That's why our recommendations only focus on those factors which showed a huge difference between low and high readership.   Bottom line: these guidelines will very likely improve your overall readership, but don't take this as gospel. Learn from your own results to refine your titles.

Methodology

We know methodology is boring, but it is also critical. You need to know how numbers and conclusions were derived, so you can have trust in them. We compared the top and bottom 25% and 33% of Dave's blog titles to find words, symbols, promises, etc. that stood out. If the differences were big enough, we included them in our recommendations.

To learn more, click here to read Deeper Approach on Methodology. You will be able to return this spot when you finish.

Chapter 3

Surprising Lessons

Dave Kerpen kindly made available data on 132 blogs he published during 2013 and 2014 (http://linkd.in/1F17n14). These blogs ranged from a low readership (Views) of 2,655 to an amazing 2,718,988! The median (more helpful considering the wide disparity in Views) was 41,191, a number most bloggers would be thrilled to have.

These blogs were written for Linked Influencer only after Dave had amassed a huge audience. At the time of this writing, Dave's followers numbered 524,838.

While the total number of his LinkedIn followers continue to increase, the number did not change significantly during this period, so more Views is not the result of a larger reader base. Dave was already one of LinkedIn's most popular bloggers. An additional interesting fact was that we found no relationship between the month the blog was published and its readership.

Our focus in this book is WHY the great disparity in Views, and how those discoveries can help you get over 100,000 readers, which Dave has done 30 times!

Following are the 7.5 Secrets that will help you improve your marketing, plus a bonus secret. All of these secrets are based on psychological research into the mind of typical buyers using an approach Dr. Witt has been using with clients and teaching university students for 20 years, *marketing psychology.* If you'd like to hear an overview and a story illustrating marketing psychology by Dr. Witt, click here for the video.

Secret 1: You have seconds to convince your reader to pay attention

Few people that you're interested in attracting have time to waste. You must grab their eyeballs and convince them you have something to offer in just a few seconds!

Lon's 1.54-Second Rule© & 5.0-Second Rule©

Lon says to understand why some words perform better that others, you must understand how we read the words and then decide if the blog, email, newspaper ad, radio or television is worth our taking the time to engage in the rest of ad. A recent study showed that today we actually have a shorter attention span than hamsters. Our headlines and title must count.

When you get your daily Google Alerts and sit down to read you daily allotment of blogs, you begin by scanning the many blog titles until one catches your eye. Our default mode is to "reject" not "read." Finally, you decide to not keep scrolling, but to click the heading for a blog.

How long do you think you were willing to spend to determine if that title was worth your time? A study showed that people are willing to spend only 1.54 seconds of time to make that determination.

Lon cautions that if a title doesn't convince you in 1.54 seconds that the time to read the blog would be worth the time invested, then you will move on to another blog. If you are listening to a commercial on the radio, watching television, or reading pages in a magazine, do you spend any longer than a second or so before either stopping or moving on? Even your Google Search results follow this 1.54 seconds rule!

Lon's 1.5 Second Rule and his 5 Second rule apply to all titles: books, white papers, case studies, your subject line in your email marketing, headlines and ads in newspapers, radio and television copy, Google searches, web pages' titles, tweets, and Facebook updates & ads, and anything written, both in traditional and digital communication.

The next hurdle you must face is the 5 Second Rule. By comparison this might sound like a lot of time, but 5 seconds isn't much time to engage your reader to stay for the full article. In fact, it's about the time it takes to read the first sentence. Your first sentences have to grab your readers and make them think the rest of your content will be as good.

If you fail with either of these two rules, your reader will move on and be lost.

Secret 2: Using the right word can make your readership explode.

The Power of Specific Words in a Title

To start out this section on the power of specific words and how we use them in advertising, listen to this amazing comedy piece from the late George Carlin in his stand up bit "Advertising Lullaby". Click now, it's worth the listen.

Let's look at Specific Words and Phrases first, then later at the use of Numbers & Symbols, Promises to Readers, Title Length, and accompanying Picture. Keep in mind this list is not definitive as it only draws on the words actually used in Dave's titles. As you learn more from you own blog's performance, add them to these lists.

We looked at 22 different words, some of them closely related, like "success" and "successful." You can view all the word in tables in the Tables section of this book.

Note: We recognize blog titles are often accompanied by a few lines of text, and that text also plays a role in creating a View. The title, however, plays the key role as it summarizes (or should) "what's in it for me," the key question the reader wants answered. The first sentence, by contrast, generally introduces the topic, which the headline has already provided. This is the 5 Second Rule©. In this book we will focus on the headline, but make some comments about the opening sentence when useful to you. You should carefully craft your opening sentence, too, to make it appealing.

Here are the words we reviewed and their ratings based on the popularity of the blogs they appeared in. If you want to see the Table data, click here:

"Success" and variants "Successful," "Succeed" - ⭐⭐⭐⭐⭐

Success is a top performing word, showing a 400% difference between its presence in the top and bottom 25% of titles, which means that while not foolproof, it gives you a distinct advantage. The reason? One obvious reason is that we all want to be successful. But, a more subtle reason is that we all want to think of ourselves as having the skills to succeed because that makes us special. Reading about "success skills" makes us believe we are growing our skills (even if we've forgotten them within the hour!)

To learn more, click Deeper Approach to read additional content.

"Inspire" and variants "Inspiration" & "Inspiring" - ⭐⭐⭐⭐

This is the only other five-star word we found in Dave's titles, showing a 300% difference between top and bottom titles (that is to say, the blogs with these words in the title appeared 3X more often in the top 25% compared to the bottom 25% of Dave's blogs ranked by readership.) As with "Success," it shows that paired with the right promise, it can be a powerhouse in getting clicks. One of Dave's best performing titles, "25 Quotes To Inspire You to

Become a Better Leader" (http://linkd.in/1BmLCVF), got over 877,000 Views! Also, "The 15 Most Inspiring Videos of All Time" (http://linkd.in/1xlmfCy) 215,513 Views (give them a listen, they are wonderful!). The lowest performer "What Inspires People" (http://linkd.in/1DhaEEN) still got 15,650 Views. To learn more, click to read Deeper Approach.

"You" and "Yours" - ⭐⭐⭐⭐

We are usually our most important concern. So anything which promises a desirable benefit for us is attractive. That's why "You" and "Yours" are high-impact words in a title. Of course, like the words above, the impact also depends on the promise. "Ways YOU Can Excel at Cricket" will have a small click-through rate in the U.S. no matter how big the word "You" is in the title. The "you" word must be accompanied by a need or desire of your readers.

"Hot" Words - ⭐⭐⭐⭐

Hot Words is our term for words which trigger a small, but important emotional response. The best examples of Hot Words, neither of which appear in these titles, are *Free* and *Sex*. The old joke that if you put them together, you've got a winning headline is actually not far from the truth. We tend to respond emotionally, that is with perked-up interest, to emotional, hot words.

The hot words identified in Dave's list are below. You'll notice that we broke out a few of them with higher usage rates for individual analysis. You might disagree with the inclusion of some words, but there are so many used that the overall findings about the value of Hot Words is not in dispute. Of course, there are many more Hot Words to use that did not appear in Dave's blogs. These just give you a sense of what types of words to look for. There are plenty of others that you can use, also. As you identify them, add them to this list for future reference as you are creating your blog title.

Note that not all of these words are four-star words, just that the composite score of all of them together adds up to a four-star category, but all are individually either three or four-star words.

List of Hot Words used in Dave's Blogs. Hot words help to grab readers' attention.

Profit	Profitable	Scariest	Secret	Success	Succeed
Successful	Opportunity	F-Word	Accomplish	Power	New
Dream	Top	Independence	Happiness	Happiest	Amazing
Trend	Incredible	Magic	Destroy	Inspiring	Future

Overall, your odds of having your blog opened increases by at least 50% if you include a Hot Word in the title. In the next chapter we'll also look at combining Hot Words.

The key in using a Hot Word is to include a word which:

- Stimulates a long-held desire or fear – like *happiness, inspiring, power, destroy, profit, independence,* etc. or
- Creates excitement by promising something "over the top," done by using hyperbole words like *amazing, incredible, magic, scary, surprisingly,* etc. or
- Promises hidden knowledge, like *secret, trends, future,* and *opportunity.*

To learn more, click <u>Deeper Approach</u> to read additional content.

"How To" - ★☆☆☆

This is a phrase which has a long history of working well in a title. See the later discussion about the Caples' book (<u>http://amzn.to/1xETSAS</u>) Tested Advertising Methods. In this analysis, the top 25% and bottom 25% both had 2 examples, while the top 33% had 4 examples, with the same two in the bottom. In short, comparing the larger lists, you double your chances of getting a click if you include "How To" paired with a desirable promise in your title.

Learn more about using "How To" in Deeper Approach by <u>clicking here</u>.

"Never" - ★☆☆☆

This might be a stronger word than 4 stars, but there are only two examples. It does not appear at all until the top 9% of the titles, where it appears twice, one pulling 609,000 Views. (<u>http://linkd.in/1KcoXiL</u>), and the other a whopping 977,000 Views (<u>http://linkd.in/1BmDODe</u>). Paired with the right fear-avoidance promise, it can be a great word in a title. For example, "Never Fear For Your Family's Safety Again!" or, "Never Lose Another Job!" Notice how the exclamation mark emphasizes the emotion. It is not used in these titles, but remains a strong symbol to use in headlines. Learn more in Deeper Approach by <u>clicking here</u>.

"Leader" - ⭐⭐☆

Leader only gets three stars, but it is not a negative word at all; it just isn't all that powerful according to the data we have analyzed, which is surprising since one of Dave's brand images as a writer is about leadership. Overall there is just one additional View in the top 25% compared to the bottom 25%. If you have a promise that involves leadership, then use it by all means, but your promise also needs to be strong – the word itself will not carry over into a click.

Here's what I mean: Dave's record-breaking title involves the term: "11 Simple Concepts To Become a Better Leader" (<u>http://linkd.in/17boYEu</u>), pulled over 2.7 million Views. Anyone who manages or hopes to manage people would be interested in this title because of the promise.

On the other hand, one of Dave's worst performing titles uses the same term: "Likeable Leader: Sushi, Sandy and Stamina" (<u>http://linkd.in/1zMBz81</u>), pulled only 6,200 Views. Other than the term *Leader* in the title, nothing else is a powerful promise, including "likeable," which isn't a major adjective for a good leader, although it does refer to Dave's books, products, and company brand.

"Secret" - ⭐⭐☆

You would think this would be a gangbuster term for a title. After all, we all love to know secrets. But, there was just one more "Secret" title in the top 25% than at the bottom, a 33% difference. Personally, I believe this is still a 4-star word, but based on the data, we'll waffle a little here. Like *Leader*, this should not dissuade you from using the term, far from it.

It may have a lower score because the term is so incredibly overused that readers have become immune to its former power. The way it works best now is if you've got a really captivating promise to go with it. It has become so ubiquitous that marketers are now even hyping the hype word – "Proven Secrets," "Undiscovered Secrets," "Simple Secrets." Soon you'll see "Really Secret Secrets." Use *secret* as you like, just make your promise is strong, clear, and highly desirable for your target market.

.

Sometimes that is difficult to tell, as Dave's third worst-performing title sounds pretty good, but "The Secret to Staying Focused On Work" (http://linkd.in/1KcqGog) pulled just 4,100 clicks. Compare that title to "9 Networking Secrets from a Superconnector" (http://linkd.in/1HuFjRA), which pulled 154,000 clicks, over 36-times the poor one. Is the latter headline 36 times better? Of course not, but that's how it worked out. You can learn more about how to tailor the promise by learning the Marketing Psychology approach to understanding buyer behavior – click here.

Just remember that "Secret" is no longer a magic word. *Hidden* is moving into the same overworked category. But, take a look at some of its synonyms which haven't gotten wide usage, like *Confidential, Private, Surprising*, or even *Personal.* You might be surprised at how well they pull. The powerful emotion all these words stimulate is the same, but others may do it more effectively than *Secret.* Learn more in Deeper Approach by clicking here.

"Jobs" or "Career" - ★★★

I suspect this is actually worth an extra star, but the usage of these terms is so low we can't award it. It was used twice in the top 33% and once in the bottom 33%. But, one of the top titles is a real ringer – "Career Highlights Won't Be on Your Tombstone" (http://linkd.in/1DlgTHS), with 149,000 Views. It has nothing to do with improving your career, but improving your life.

Career is not ever going to be a steamroller word, but it promises readers some help with their job or career, something of importance to most readers. The title would be more powerful if it focused on not losing a job, a big fear for many. In general, research shows we are more fearful of losing what we already have than of gaining something new. Remember to incorporate that idea into some of your blog titles, such as "Three Big Ways You'll Lose Money When Selling Your House!" You should not hesitate to use *jobs* or *career*, but you'll need to carefully pair it with a clear, strong promise your readers want.

"Lessons" or "Tips" - ★★★

These words aren't used much in Dave's titles, a total of 4 times, evenly balanced between the top and bottom 33%. Readers like to see them because they promise some short and simple ideas for making improvements, such as "Tips on Tipping" or "Simple Lessons for Investing."

Usually these words are paired with some number, like "6 Tips…" and that is likely the best way to use them as they don't have the strength to carry a title on their own. You could include *Rules* in this list, too. If the blog title were compared to a film, these words would be supporting actors.

"Best" & "Most" - ☆☆☆

No difference in the top and bottom 33% for use of these words. As with "Tips," these words are supporting actors. They, and many others like them, are used to enhance the power of some noun – "The Best-Paying Companies in America" could be appealing to readers, while "The Best Day of My Life" not so much. All the three-star words can be useful for pulling in readers, but only as an adjective or enhancer to more important words and to the overall promise.

"Simple" - ☆☆☆

This is a surprising finding considering that we all like "simple" ideas. But, the word *simple* was used in six different titles, 3 in the top 33% and 3 in the bottom 33%. It had one more use in the bottom 25% versus the top 25% of titles. In other words, it is not a word you can trust to deliver a View. While the word itself is attractive, it may well have become so overused in titles of all kinds that it has lost its individual power. Don't be afraid to use it with other strong words and a good promise. After all, Dave's 2.7 million view title was "11 Simple Concepts to become a Better Leader" (http://linkd.in/17boYEu).

· · · · · · · · · · · · · · · ·

Summary of Findings on Words Used in Blog Titles

The strongest words based on this analysis of 133 titles are

- "Success" and its variants
- "Inspire" and its variants
- "You" and "Yours"
- Hot words that convey or create emotion in one of three ways:
1. Stimulates a long-held desire or fear – like happiness, inspiring, power, destroy, profit, independence, etc.
2. Creates excitement by promising something "over the top," done by using hyperbole words like amazing, incredible, magic, scary, surprisingly, etc.
3. Promises hidden knowledge, like secret, trends, future, opportunity.
- "How To"
- "Never"

There are a number of "helper" words which lend greater impact to strong words. Many of the words found in the Hot Words category fall into this list. These words can't carry a title, but can boost interest....

- "Job" and "Career"
- "Leader"
- "Secret" (also a strong word)
- "Lessons" and "Tips"
- "Best" and "Most"
- "Simple" (despite its slightly negative data, it is clearly an attractive helper word).
- "Hot Words" like Dream, Top, Amazing, Trend, Magic, Opportunity, Future, etc.

Using several positive key words in a title increases the Views, as does avoiding negative key words.

Secret 3: Your opening sentence is for Marketing, not information!

Opening Sentences of the Blog

Opening sentences, which sometimes appear below the blog title, have only one value. They are the back-up to lure readers into opening the blog if the title alone did not do it. These sentences should be viewed as a marketing tool to reinforce the title and gain a click, NOT as the start of your blog. They should be a "come on" to interest readers.

Don't waste this important real estate on some traditional opening, which generally just sets the stage for the blog's information. Instead, use the words and other elements we cover in this book to make a second pitch to the readers, trying to get them to commit to reading your blog. For example, in a blog titled "What Are You Really Selling?" my opening line was "You may think you know what you are selling, but you're almost certainly wrong. How do you discover the answer? Start here."

Don't disregard this Secret! A great title can be diminished or even destroyed by a boring opening. For example, "The Best Clothing for Sophisticated Seduction" is likely to pull in readers, but this opening is a real turn-off: "In 1348 the King of England and the Catholic Church laid down some rules about fashion..." Just remember, the first couple of lines of your blog should be considered part of your marketing Title, the way a tagline is part of a brand name.

In the next chapter we will look at symbols and numbers used in titles. You may be surprised at some of the findings!

Chapter 4

Numbers, Symbols, & Multiple Key Words

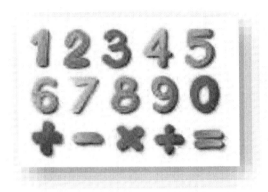

While we may put a lot of thought into the title words we use, numbers and especially symbols don't get much thought. But, that kind of thinking turns out to be a big mistake, at least so far as our analysis of Dave's 132 titles go.

Secret 4: Numbers and Symbols can boost or bust your readership!

You'll find a summary of our individual findings below. If you want to learn more, follow the links to Deeper Approach and visit the tables in the appendix.

We also looked at how titles performed when multiple key words were used together, including with symbols. We'll look at the power of numbers first.

If you want to see the Table data for this chapter, click here:

Numbers - ☆☆☆☆☆

Turns out that numbers are one of the most powerful items you can include in your title. There is a 113% difference between the Views in the top vs. bottom 25% directly related to numbers. 17 titles out of 33 in the top 25% use numbers – over half of the most successful titles include a number! This holds true for the top 33% as well. Exactly 50% of those titles start with or include a number.

When we interviewed people to find out why numbered lists performed better, we found that most said things like "I can do '5 Steps', I will skim the '10 Things', I want to know what the '15 Don'ts' are, I have time for that. I don't have time to read a book or even a long blog, but I can read a few bullet points." Like most of us, your readers don't have much time, but they do crave helpful information. Learn more in our Deeper Approach.

Types of Numbers

We wondered if any particular elements in numbers made them more appealing to readers. It is a well-known and not understood belief among comics that certain numbers are funnier in a joke than others, and that odd numbers are funnier than even numbers.

Odd vs. Even Numbers

Odd numbers appeared 4X as often as even numbers, but there was no difference in their power to pull in a view. In fact, even numbers had a higher percentage of top versus bottom 33% titles than odd numbers. Bottom line: We see no practical difference in using odd or even numbers in your titles. Learn more about using odd and even numbers in Deeper Approach.

Size of Numbers

Numbers specify the size of the list readers will confront. A list of 3 steps seems a lot more manageable than a list of 27 steps. It seemed reasonable that the smaller the number, the more attractive the blog might be. This was not the case.

These results show any number, single or double digit, about equally improves your chances of having your blog opened. Given the high use of numbers in Dave's blog titles, it would appear that the View value (percentage who click on View) of the number may even be somewhat independent of the type of list promised. Bottom line: Lots of people are using numbers in their headlines – because they work. You should, too. But, remember that we may be getting to the point where numbers are so overused that they go the way of "secret" and "simple." It is also worth considering your own reaction to titles with big numbers versus small numbers -- personally, I'll open a blog with 3 tips over one with 99 tips.

On the technical side, a number placed in front of the title and not a character (any letter, *a* through *z*), always pushes the title to the top of a list of titles. Computers use ASCII codes a three digit number between 001 and 255 to internally represent all characters, numbers, symbols, and hidden characters. In the list of ASCII codes, numbers come before alphabetical characters. This title will always appear at the top when sorted by title. (See http://ascii.cl/)

Question Mark (?) - ☆☆☆
While this showed up with a one-star rating, our analysis concludes this is only based on Dave's uninspired question titles. We think that rank is an anomaly and the use of question marks in titles should have at least three-stars, as shown here, or even four.

Questions are a common form of headline, such as *"Do you suffer from these pains?"*

Advertisers swear by questions in headlines as they force a sub-conscience response, and thus an engagement, from the reader. For example, *"Have You Ever Misplaced Your Cell Phone?"* created an immediate answer in your mind. If you have, you may be interested in how to avoid it again, and if you haven't, you'll want to know how to never lose your phone. Direct marketers have long known that finding the right type of question is critical for a good pull. That was Dave's problem here.

In analyzing Dave's headlines, not one "question" headline appears in the top 25%, and only one appeared in the top 33%; however, 8 "question" headlines rank in the bottom third. Want to know why? To find out, read more in our Deeper Approach. After careful analysis and research, we recommend you go with the pros' experience and use question marks in your titles. But, ONLY if you are stimulating a strong interest motivation. See what you think by reading more in Deeper Approach, click here.

Number of Words in Headline - ☆☆
Most of Dave's titles are short, under 7 words. Some studies have found significance in the number of words in a headline. We didn't find that here when looking at these short titles, mostly six words and under. We compared the top and bottom halves of the list, finding 17 short titles in the top list and 14 in the bottom, not enough difference for any significance.

In a study by Outbrain, titles with exactly 8 words got 21% more click-throughs. In our analysis, 12% of the titles in the bottom third had 8 words in the title, while 21% of the top third of titles used 8 words, a meaningful spread. There also seems to be a natural rhythm to most of the 8-word titles in the top third, what poets call meter, which is far less present in the lower titles using 8 words. That rhythm, although read silently, may have something to do with the harmoniousness of the title, but it could also just be a coincidence. Don't know what a "meter" is? Just recite "Mary had a little lamb" and you'll hear the rhythm of how you are saying the words. That rhythm is pleasing to the mind.

Bottom line, use the fewest words you need to clearly get your promise across. If you can work out a nicely flowing, rhythmic title of 8 words that makes a strong promise, it's worth trying, but I wouldn't bet on 8 words being a key factor,   either.

Colon (:) - ☆
Colons are used when the author wants to put two related ideas together, such as "Cell Phone Plans: Best and Worst Compared." The copy after the title is equivalent to a tagline for the prior words. Colons are used 13 times in the top and bottom 33% of titles. Of those 13 times, 12 appear in the bottom third of all title Views! That is a significant difference, even with a relatively small sample. For some reason, colons seem to turn people off. Bottom line, stay away from colons, they are one of the clearest danger signals we found.

Combinations: Presence of Key Words and Symbols in Titles
We've seen the impact of individual words and symbols in titles. Often, titles will include more than one of these key words or symbols, so it is important to look at the impact of multiples indicators. As seen in the tables (click here) , the top titles use twice as many positive key words (those

33

with 3 stars and above) as negative key words (below 3 stars). Loading a title with more than one positive key word, and even more so avoiding negative key words, is a good way to create Views.

You can see the results of a set of positive key words versus a set of negative key words in Table 4 by clicking here.

Summary of Recommendations in this Chapter

- Use numbers in your titles. Odd or even doesn't matter, nor does the size of the number.
- Avoid colons (:) in your titles.
- Despite the findings, use question marks, there are too many positive findings about them over past decades of testing to avoid using them.
- Length of the title doesn't seem to have any effect, but another study found 8 words was a good length.
- Use multiple positive key words to increase your chance of a view
- Make sure any three-star key word is paired with a very strong promise.

Chapter 5
Promises in Titles

The words in titles are important, as we've seen. But, the value of words is in the interest they create in the reader's mind. If they are related to something the reader needs, wants, fears or desires, the title will grab attention. If not, your blog will be passed by.

For example, if I'm interested in refinancing my house and a title says *Don't Make These ReFi Mistakes!* I'll likely read it. The title has reminded me of a fear, the fear of making a mistake and losing money. I will take the time to read articles promising to show me how to avoid mistakes. Good titles seduce the reader by making promises that readers want. Good titles are psychologically seductive.

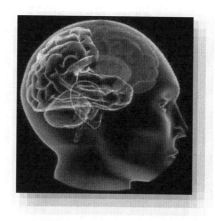

To learn more, click Deeper Approach and read about Dr. Witt's proven approach to designing all marketing promises -- Buyer Motivation Analysis. Deeper Approach.

If you'd like to hear more about marketing psychology, listen to Dr. Witt explain his psychological approach to customer seduction by

checking out this video:
https://www.youtube.com/watch?v=V-JfCQXEi10.

We looked at Dave's titles to see what sort of promises they made. The more important the promise is to a reader, the more likely the blog will be read.

After some analysis, we saw there were basically three types of headlines used:

.

1. Titles that promised improvement in yourself
2. Titles that promised improvement in your skills
3. Titles that offered unfocused promises, confusing promises, and no promises

The results are fascinating and clear cut. We can sum them up in the next Secret:

Secret 5: Make concrete promises that will improve the reader.

The worst-performing titles offered unfocused, confusing or no promises. This clearly shows people want Promises that offer specific benefits and satisfactions.

The results also show that people find it more valuable to improve themselves than their skills. As you see in <u>Table #3,</u> "improve <u>yourself</u>" promise titles show up **three time more often at the top** than "improve your <u>skills</u>" titles. It may be that many already believe they have sufficient skills in that area.

Readers apparently feel they can benefit from self-improvement. For example, a typical self-improvement title at the top (378,000 Views) is *How To Turn Weaknesses into Strengths*, (http://linkd.in/1D7ydCT). This is appealing because we all have weaknesses and want strengths. By contrast, a low-value (and confusing) self-improvement title promised *15 Ways to Get You Unstuck* (http://linkd.in/1Aomcp7), with 5,200 Views.

If you have a blog which does improve some skill sets, the results suggest you are better off finding a title which relates your deliverables to self-improvement. For example, one of Dave's improve-your-skills titles is *7 Simple Rules for Amazing Content Marketing*, (http://linkd.in/1F5Y6EU) with only 47,100 Views. It could have been a self-improvement title like *How To Become a Great Content Writer.* We are more interested in ourselves than in how we do our job.

Remember, a self-help promise title is not a guarantee, but it will more than double your odds of a click over a skills-based promise according to the data analyzed. And, it will give you a **500% greater chance of a View** over a headline which has a confusing, unfocused promise, or no promise at all. It's really all about playing the odds to get the numbers you want!

Fear-Related Promises In Titles

Fear is one of the marketer's greatest friends. People fear or can be seduced into fearing so many things, fears which can then be eliminated by buying products or services or even ideas. From your dandruff shampoo to your CPA to your insurance policies to your vote, you buy many things in hopes of reducing your fears about something that may happen.

Fears are, of course, emotions. You can read much more about positive (desires) and negative (fears) emotions in the Deeper Approach.

I want to take a special look at fear titles, not just in Dave's list, but others as well because they are such a powerful way of attracting readers. One reason is our fear of loss. **Most of us fear losing what we have more than we desire to gain something new. Marketers use that to their advantage.**

Dave makes little use of fear-based titles, but when he does, they pay off. In the bottom third of his blogs he uses two, both of them just "on the line" scary, like *9 of the Scariest Business Stories You'll Ever Hear* (http://bit.ly/1Vy2rFv, 10,867 views.)" In the top third, he has only two genuinely fear-related titles, *5 Google Results That Can Destroy Your Career* (http://bit.ly/1P8RmFK, 200,330 views) and his second-highest scorer, *17 Things You Should Never Say to Your Boss* (http://bit.ly/1MNbRJe, 977,379). Even two examples shows the power of fear in a blog title.

Here are some other very good examples of fear-related titles. What do you think they have in common?

7 Dangerous Decisions That Ruin Careers Before They Begin
7 Bad Habits to Drop If You Want to be Successful
6 Ways 99% of People Are Destroying Their Careers
6 LinkedIn Opportunities You're Missing Out On
4 Words That RUIN Your Personal Brand
4 Things That Destroy Job Interviews

I'll bet that you would like to read several of them. Why? Because we all fear doing something wrong that will hurt us. Notice how important the verbs are in most of these titles – "destroy," "ruin," "missing." **Strong, fear-provoking verbs are great for grabbing attention and raising fears.** Here are some more: Spoil, cripple, wipe out, defeat, fail, suffer, flop, disappoint, fire, fall, crash. You also noticed the use of numbers in those titles to lure readers with the promise of a fast read.

But powerful verbs and numbers are only part of the formula for good fear-related titles or headlines.

Here are 7 guidelines for using fear in a title:

1. Determine something that your target readers would hate to lose, something important to them.

2. Pick a short, concrete noun to express that thing – not "employment" but "job," for example. Remember what Winston Churchill said, *Old words are best, and old words, when they are short words, are best of all.*

3. Pick a strong, meaningful verb, one that is loaded with associated emotions, like "lost."

4. Bait your title with a personalized idea that will make them afraid it could come true, like this picture's headline.

5. Make sure your title is focused on something THEY are doing or not doing. If it is not under their control, it isn't what you want in your title. *5 Ways Your Company Could Fail* is no good, but *7 Ways You Are Crippling Your Career* works well.

6. Make your title short, very clear and focused on what they will lose, like a threat.

7. Use a picture that visually enhances their fear, like the one below.

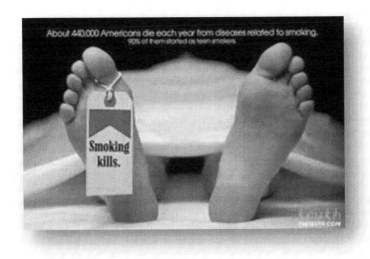

Remember that readers are clicking for only one reason – to find out HOW to avoid losing. If you've made me afraid that I'm doing something at work which could cost me my job or image, then when I look at your blog, you better be telling me exactly what it is and how to stop doing it.

Don't 'bait-and-switch' readers or give them some pabulum blog with abstract or general ideas. Your job is to deliver the goods you promise – or they will never trust you again.

For example, let's say your blog is on good business communication skills. These are skills that most bosses want and many employees are sorely lacking. So for the concrete noun we could use "job," but let's use "promotion."

It is legitimate to think a person without strong interpersonal skills could lose their chance at a promotion. So for our verb, we could use "lose," but something strong would be better, like "squander."

We want to make our title fearful, and based on something they are doing now. If they are messing up, then we can easily say they are making "mistakes," another fear-laden term.

So, our short title might then be *Are You Squandering Your Chance for Promotion With These 5 Mistakes?* We use a question, a number, a hot word and two strong fear words, a good combo. This is a good example of how you can use this book to carefully construct your headline like you were using Lego blocks.

Finally, look for a good picture that reinforces the fear in some visual way. The picture will help them to remember your blog, too.

To create any fear-related title, follow this blueprint and make sure you can say "yes" to each of the 7 guidelines listed above. You will find that fear is your friend, too.

By the way, pay attention to print and television ads you see that have a fear component in them. Analyze what they do – then use those lessons yourself.

Chapter 6

Pictures

Decades of research has proven beyond doubt the importance of pictures in any advertisement. We are visual animals. We look at pictures first.

Of course, pictures, like words, are different. Some pictures are great and others are lousy at generating the interest you need. The job of the picture is to grab attention and stimulate interest. In a magazine ad, for example, if the picture does not immediately grab the reader's interest in some way, the page is turned and the opportunity is lost – along with the money paid for that potential exposure to a new customer.

Here is a great picture used by e-Harmony.com. Its target market are people who want a lasting

1) Good picture = people enjoying
Thanks — a kid & mum — lovers
a kid.

relationship. The picture grabs attention and stimulates interest by showing readers exactly what they long for – true love. Think of all the other pictures that could be used; a wedding cake, a bridal bouquet, two glasses of champagne, etc. None of them are nearly as good as this picture, because this picture shows readers the image already in their minds, the loving couple, what they desire to become. **That's the core lesson of marketing psychology – show the person what their heart and mind desires, the satisfaction they want**.

The eye's natural progression is from the picture to the headline. This is a perfect headline for the picture because it reinforces the promise that the reader wants; someone with whom to spend the rest of their lives with, "Everlasting Love." Your blog title should do the same with the promise it makes the reader.

Secret 6: The Right Picture Grabs Eyeballs and Generates Views.

The right picture stops traffic, while the poorer picture, like a champagne flute, will not. If the reader is not stopped, the headline and copy are not read, and the opportunity of a sale is lost. All because of a lousy picture! Your blog can overcome the handicap of a bad picture or even no picture, but your odds of gaining a reader are greater with a good picture. Think of your picture and its headline as the bait for your blog. To learn more about using pictures, go to Deeper Approach.

In analyzing Dave's images, we found his pictures had no benefit at all. This has nothing to do with the value of pictures, but with the value of the particular pictures selected. Pictures are not magic. Some help, some hurt, and most are just neutral, like most of his.

Looking at some representative pictures can be instructive. Below you'll find several of Dave's blog titles along with its accompanying picture and its total views. These offer some typical examples of each category of images, moving from lowest to most Views. See what you think. Which of the pictures would capture your attention by themselves? Do you see any difference between those at the bottom and those at the top of list?

These picture selections generally make perfect sense in relation to the title. They just aren't very helpful in grabbing interest or making a promise. Pictures need to stimulate a need, a promise, or a benefit, just like headlines, to grab eyeballs.

Dave's blog titles and pictures:

Simple Ways You Can Get More Out of Conferences (the blog's headline)
3,306 Views
(http://linkd.in/1wOIQIu)
There is nothing inherently interesting in a sea of people, and the image doesn't make sense until <u>after</u> you look at the headline! Remember the picture is selected to stop readers and get them to look at the headline. Here the eyes just bounce off.

1.5 Million Reasons Social Media Is Key For Your Business
6,819 Views
(http://linkd.in/1w5VOfM)
Above are a group of likeable people you don't know and can barely see, so there is no push to read the headline. The very small curiosity factor here of what they are doing is not nearly enough to compel a reader to take the time to click and read. It is not enough to make readers mildly wonder "What is going on here?" The intensity of that wonder must be strong enough to propel them to read the headline to find out, to satisfy their curiosity. They have other things to do with their time, so the curiosity must be strong enough to make them willing to give up a little

more time to discover the answer. That is always the trade-off.

Turn Your Job Into Your Dream Career
37,947 Views
(http://linkd.in/1D7zklY)
We see an attractive woman looking at us, which will catch our attention (we look at people who are looking at us, especially attractive ones). But, that's as far as this image goes. There is no stimulation of a need, want, fear or desire, no curiosity, nothing. It is just a placeholder picture that has nothing to do with the title. (You'll see a similar picture further below that has a great tie to the headline and really pulled in the views!)

How to Achieve Career Independence
45,238 Views
(http://linkd.in/1HuOQYX)
This picture of a word illustrates the title. The strong colors and single, emotion-laden word may grab some initial attention. A slight curiosity factor may lead to a glance at the headline. The headline then delivers a reasonably strong promise, enough to get 45,000 Views. A typically illustrative, two to three-star picture, nothing more.

5 Google Results That Can Destroy Your Career

211,488 Views
(http://linkd.in/1IcZP7O)
Here is another typical placeholder picture. A million other pictures would have done as well, as it has nothing to do with the blog title. We don't know why this guy is smiling, especially since his career may be destroyed! The pictures has only one value – the guy is looking at the reader with both eyes, which tends to attract attention. It was enough. Readers looked at the headline, their fear level was raised, and the blog was a winner. The great phrase "destroy your career" created fear, and a desire to find out how to avoid this unknown problem.

The One thing a Num must do

The One Thing a Business Leader Must Do
306,608 Views
(http://linkd.in/14nnOEQ)
This is a tremendously weak picture except for one feature; it is an eye-grabbing orange. On the other hand, the headline is relatively strong, leading to over 306,000 Views. We suspect it may be the combination of the words "one" and "must." It seems worth a few seconds to find out what this one critical action is, just in case it is important.

How This 32-Year Old Twitter Employee Has a 21-Year Old Son
723,818 Views
(http://linkd.in/14nnZQu)
The picture below has the benefit of an attractive face staring out at you – we look at people who are looking at us. It was enough to glance at the headline, back at the woman, and think "No way!" The combination of the picture and the headline create great curiosity, which can only be answered by viewing the blog. And, nearly 724,000 people did.

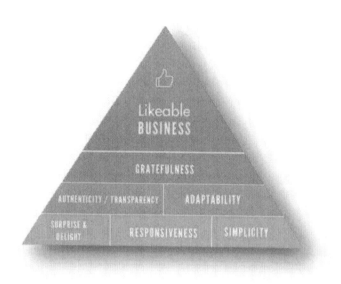

11 Simple Concepts to Become a Better Leader
2,730,184 Views
(http://linkd.in/17boYEu)
Here's the big winner, the off-the-charts View leader
– close to 3 million people viewed this blog! Why?

As you can see, the picture is illustrative at best, has
no people in it, and half the words are hard to read.
The only positive is its likeable orange color and
some words that have positive associations, like
passion and *storytelling.*

Irrespective, readers looked at the title and it sold
them. Dave is known as a leadership guru, and the
headline promises some easy ideas to improve that
skill. Note also that the headline does not promise
to improve your leadership skills, but to make you a
better leader. The viewership is so far off the curve
that its performance was likely an anomaly that

would not repeat this level of performance, but should still pull many Views because of the strong promise headline.

The point of these illustrations is to show that while blog titles can be successful without a strong image (if you are Dave Kerpen!), the average blogger will benefit by using strong images to enhance the pulling power of their blog title. Also remember that Dave had a loyal audience to start with. If you don't, you need all the help you can get! Spending extra time to find a great image for your headline can really pay off in more Views for your blog. To learn more about the psychology of good pictures, read Deeper Approach.

As you select your picture, remember these ideas:

1. A meaningless, generic image is the worst one you can pick. It does nothing to capture attention and often confuses the reader since it has nothing to do with the title. Think of the picture and headline together as one piece of bait for the reader.

2. An image which illustrates the topic is OK. It just won't help you much. The illustration simply tells the audience the topic the blog will discuss.

3. An image which is illustrative and provokes curiosity can be strong because people who are curious want answers. But you need to build strong curiosity!

4. An image which is illustrative and funny can be strong because it suggests the blog will be an entertaining read. Laughter is an "added value" that attracts people to your blog. That is why funny

things are the most popular "shares" or e-mail forwards to friends.

5. An image which is both illustrative and shows a benefit the reader wants is best of all. **People do not want what you are pushing, even a free blog.** They want some **satisfaction**, such as helpful knowledge, entertainment, emotional growth, power, wealth, time, stress reduction, comfort, self-esteem, etc. **That is what you need to promise them with your picture and title. Then deliver in your blog.**

BONUS SECTION: Learn a lot more about how to select pictures that really do help sell. There is a psychological science to it which you'll be introduced to in this Deeper Approach.

Chapter 7

Blogs & Social

In this chapter, Lon shows you in blogging there are two other very important statistics you need to consider after you've gotten your reader to view your blog -- Comments and Likes / Shares.

Secret 7: Push readers to comment, Like and Share or you are wasting half the power of your blog.

Engagement, the Call To Comment

Blog sites, LinkedIn, and Facebook all allow reader comments to blogs or updates. When they comment on your content, it really engages your readers and gets them involved. This gives them a perceived partial ownership and encourages them to promote your content to others. A very clever way to encourage comments on your blog is to ask a couple of questions at the end.

Dave really "engages" his audience and encourages comments with closing questions using an ending section he calls "Now It's Your Turn". Engaging people brings them closer to your brand and they feel a part of your success. Deliberately asking questions at the end of your blog reminds and encourages them to participate. Brilliant!

Here are several examples of Dave's call to comment:

"Now it's your turn": Have you ever listened to a podcast? What podcasts do you love? Which have helped you become a better leader? Does your company have a podcast? If not, what's stopping you from starting one?" And...

"Now it's your turn": What companies do you think do a great job of being helpful or useful? What is your "Youtility"? What useful information do you provide to your customers and prospects? And, how do you get the word out about it through social media? Please let me know in the Comments section below, and please do share this post with your network." And...

"Now it's your turn": Which of these leadership principles are most important to you? What attributes would you add? What makes you a likeable leader? Share your thoughts in the comment section below!

The analysis showed blogs with the highest Engagement were about family and work, problems we all face, and the blogs on How To. It was the social side of the conversation getting the best engagement, not the numbered lists. This makes sense as a list is a list; a quick way to digest information and move on. The social side encouraged conversation. So, do you want engagement or just views?

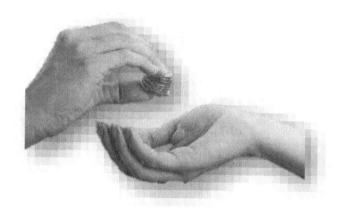

Likes & Shares Equal Trust

When someone hits "Share" on your blog, this allows others in each of their networks to see your content. This is the Holy Grail of blogging. By successfully getting your reader to Like or Share your content, you can get in front of multiples of new readers. "Shares" can change the number of readers you have exponentially.

If your title is engaging and your content is so good readers want to share, you could increase your viewership to over one million readers with a few clicks.

The blogs with titles such as Reality TV, 21 Favorite Songs, or Negative Workplace had the least Likes per view. Another interesting statistic was, as the

Views increased, the likes went down. It may be that Dave's core readers are more likely to take time to Like his blog than more casual readers, or that he was turning former Likes into Comments.

Getting "shares" is a function of trust -- trust in you and your content. Remember when someone shares your content with their tribe, sharing is a reflection on them. Good content, secrets, tips, to do's, what to avoid, and how to's will make them look good to their network. In a way, they get credit for bringing good content to their readers.

Sharing also makes them feel good about themselves – they have enriched their friends or co-workers in some way with new ideas, information, humor, or pictures. Since we like to feel that way, we will want to do it again, so your reminder to

"Share" may be just the little reminder they need to do it.

Don't be afraid to ask your readers to like / share your blogs. They won't think of it unless you remind them. **Always ask your readers (customers) to do what you want them to do next.** Don't count on them to know what you want. Get them to share your content.

The Importance of Signature Blocks

Dave is brilliant using his signature block at the end of every blog. It summarizes every take-away he wants to leave with his reader. Notice how he uses the final text block plus image as a way of asking the readers to engage with him again,

Here's an example:

"Dave Kerpen is the founder and CEO of Likeable Local. He is also the cofounder and Chairman of Likeable Media, and the New York Times bestselling author of Likeable Social Media and Likeable Business, and the new collection, Likeable Leadership (http://amzn.to/1BmQ0Uy). To read more from Dave on LinkedIn, please click the FOLLOW button above or below.

Want to learn about how to grow your business using social media in 2 minutes? Check out this video. (http://hub.am/1nBbtnt)"

This block shows Dave's readers his accomplishments, promotes his book, and his company. It also encourages readers to connect with him on LinkedIn and drives people to his web site with a tantalizing promise of spending only 2 minutes to benefit from his expertise. Anyone can spare 2 minutes to learn more after reading a helpful blog.

What is even more important, using your "keywords" in your signature block reinforces these words with the search engines. It strengthens your page index for those keywords.

When Best To Publish

When I spoke with Dave about what he felt was the best time to publish a blog, he recommended Monday - Wednesday in the AM EST.

It turns out that Dave is right again. To be very specific, **studies have shown that both email blasts and blog postings are the most effective when sent at 10:00 AM on Tuesday** followed by 10:00 AM on Thursday, followed by 10:00 on Wednesday. For more information on when and why timing is important, read Lon's *The Social Media Bible.*

Chapter 7.5

Luck!

The Final Ingredient In Getting 2 Million Views

We all know that preparation is key to success. In Malcolm Gladwell's book <u>*Outliers*</u>, he suggests that roughly 10,000 hours of focused practice is needed to develop any natural skills or abilities you might have to the point where you could be successful. That's a lot of preparation.

Many people define success as "Where preparation meets opportunity". But, that is not always the case. At one time or another, we have been very prepared when an opportunity presented itself, but the results were far less than anticipated or we even went away empty-handed.

After speaking with and interviewing so many successful people, all admitted coming to the same conclusion – luck plays a big part in any success.

BONUS SECRET (#7.5: You Need Luck to Hit the Homeruns!

Dave himself said it in his email... It's all about luck! "Success is where preparation meets opportunity, <u>and</u> you get struck by luck."

If you're not prepared or opportunity never knocks, you won't see success. Even if both are true, there is no guarantee of success unless lucky lightning strikes. We all know supremely smart and talented people with great ideas who are still struggling unknowns.

Dave Kerpen told Lon "I've had posts that have had as few as 2K views and posts with as many as 2M views, so obviously there are other factors, including luck, at play."

So... Be prepared! (This book will help.) Wait for your   opportunity!   And...
Keep your fingers crossed!

Chapter 8

Summary & Conclusions

We hope this book has helped you better understand the important elements in titles and pictures as you make those important decisions for your own blogs.

These guidelines are far from foolproof, and are based on business-related blogs. If you are blogging about quilting or baby care, we believe you'll have a similar experience, but make sure you **keep records to learn what works for you**.

This book should give you some good ideas about how to analyze each element of your blogs. The more unknowns you can eliminate and the more educated guesses you can make, the greater your success.

Of course, the starting point for any blog is its **content.** There must be something in it that people will want to read – otherwise, why would you bother to write it? So that's the core around which you select the elements with which to build your title, then select your picture.

All of this analysis led us to develop the **7 Secrets** you saw in the text. Now here they all are together. If you follow the first 7 as you prepare your blog, you will develop more readers, more Likes, and a better chance at getting Lucky!

Secret 1: You have only seconds to convince your reader to pay attention.

Secret 2: Using exactly the right word in your title can make your readership explode.

Secret 3: Your opening sentence is for Marketing, not information!

Secret 4: Numbers and symbols can boost or bust your readership!

Secret 5: Make concrete promises that improve the reader

Secret 6: The right picture grabs eyeballs and generates views.

Secret 7: Push readers to Comment, Like and Share or you are wasting half the power of your blog.

Bonus Secret 7.5: You need luck to hit the home runs!

Average success is where preparation meets opportunity. Amazing success is where preparation meets opportunity and is struck by the lightening of luck. Without preparation or an opportunity, you cannot have success. For over-the-top success, you still need luck.

Here is a brief summary of some of the key findings all in one spot for easy reference.

Individual Words in Your Title

- **Words that are strong by themselves and attract readers**

✓ Success, Successful, Succeed, and similar words
✓ Inspire, Inspiration, Inspiring, and similar words
✓ You, Yours - remember, in your reader's mind, it really is "all about me!"
✓ How To, Never, Secret!

- **Hot Words – words that convey emotion, positive or negative:**

Profit	Profitable	Scariest	Secret	Success	Succeed
Successful	Opportunity	F-Word	Accomplish	Power	New
Dream	Top	Independence	Happiness	Happiest	Amazing
Trend	Incredible	Magic	Destroy	Inspiring	Future

- **Words that help strong words be stronger**

○ Leader
○ Lessons or Tips
○ Best and Most
○ Secret (also a strong word)
○ Simple

Symbols & Numbers

- Numbers are powerful, big or small, odd or even.
- Ask a question, and don't forget the question mark.
- Avoid colons, one of our strongest findings.
- Length of the title doesn't seem to matter, use the fewest words to make a clear promise.
- Multiple positive key words in a title perform better in general than just one. Pair them with a strong word.

Promises

- In Marketing Psychology, there are four major categories of motivation – Needs, Wants, Fears and Desires. The first two are logical and the last two are emotional. Together they form a marketer's Buyer Motivation Analysis, the matrix of satisfactions that is the first step in picking a title and picture. We make choices based on both emotion and logic.

- Titles promising self-improvement generated over twice as many Views as titles promising skill improvement.

- Promises which were unfocused or confusing performed very poorly.

- Titles with no promises performed very poorly, too.

- Make promises in your title based on the strongest motivators of your target readers.

Pictures

- Based on much research, pictures are very important for the performance of any marketing print piece, from ads to blogs.

- Pictures should make a promise the reader wants. It should be clear and simple.

- People look at pictures first, then the title or headline. You need a picture that grabs readers by stimulating curiosity or making a promise they want.

- _____

-

- Whenever possible, the headline should reinforce the promise in the picture.

- Close-ups in which a person stares out at the reader are proven "stoppers."

- An image which creates strong curiosity in the reader is good.

- An image which makes the reader laugh is good if it leads to a click.

- An image which shows happy people using the product is proven successful.

<u>Social Aspects</u>

- Engagement with readers once they have opened the blog is important. A great way is to ask readers to offer their own comments, share their own experiences. It is important to be clear that you want them to reply. It is also important to ask them to share your blog with others if they liked it.

- If you want to build a loyal reader base, you must gain their trust. Always tell the truth, don't hype yourself too much, give them information they can use and confidently pass along to their tribe, and always try to give them more than they expect.

- Your signature block is a social element. It should not only tell them who you are, what you do and what you sell, but also invite them to contact you, to establish a longer-term relationship. Don't forget to include a picture there, like a book, that helps to emphasize your brand image. And be sure to ask them to comment!

- Everyone is busy and your blog is just another intrusion asking for time and attention. If you are liked and trusted, you'll get their time. But try to be a good friend by dropping your blog on them at times when it will have the best chance of being opened. So plan your calendar each week so it is ready to go on time.

- Research suggests that Monday through Wednesday in the mornings are good times, with Tuesday at 10:00 a.m. (reader's time) the optimum moment.

Luck

- Luck is the extra added ingredient, the 0.5 that gives you the edge. Even Dave agrees that his 2.7 million reader blog was in part luck.

- You can't count on luck; you can only count on being prepared when it shows up.

- Remember the old and true adage, Preparation + Luck = Success. A variation says Luck is when Preparation meets Opportunity. In any case, luck won't do you any good if you are not prepared for it.

- If your preparation requires marketing, social media, or fusion marketing advice, Gary and Lon are at your service. If you need help on leadership, Dave is ready to serve you. You may find that reading this book was a stroke of luck!

In closing, remember that what you do and what you say is a reflection of your personality. If you want others to like, trust and admire you as a stellar person, then you must treat them with honesty, respect, friendship and kindness. Ultimately, the most successful interactions come when two people are trying to help each other.

Acknowledgements

We would like to thank Dave Kerpen for allowing us to take such a detailed and candid look at all of his great content on LinkedIn and for his support in the production of this book.

We would also like to thank all of the Google Image contributors for the use of their images under Creative Commons (http://www.creativecommons.org). If there is any image someone wishes we don't use in this publication, please notify one of us authors and it will be removed immediately.

Bonus Material:

Fusion Marketing

Bonus Material: Fusion Marketing

While the full power of the Fusion Marketing concept from *The Fusion Marketing Bible* published by McGraw Hill is beyond the scope of this book, it is important to understand it's basic ideas. [http://www.TheFusionMarketingBible.com]

Fusion Marketing is a system that allows you to analyze all of your traditional marketing, your digital marketing, and your social media marketing. From that analysis, you determine what's working and what's not, eliminate what isn't working, and combine and **completely integrate** all of the most successful tools for your company, products, and service. This integration can save you money, improve your ROI, discover new marketing combinations, and impress your customers. It also allows you to create a great marketing plan.

The Safko Wheel, which
is really 3 movable,
interlocking wheels

By using the, **Safko Marketing Wheel** (U.S. Patent Pending) you:

1. Identify all traditional marketing you have used in the past.

2. Identify which traditional tools have been effective through the use of "Cost of Customer Acquisition".

3. Identify which digital and social media tools are right for you and your marketing plan.

4. Select and completely integrate the best tools for you from the three marketing tool categories.

5. Inter-connect each and every tool to each other tool to significantly increase the effectiveness of each tool.

6. Look at each selected tool individually and create a program to enhance the effectiveness of each tool.

7. Create multiple objectives.

8. And, by creating just 5 Objectives and using only 20 tools, you can generate 100 tactics.

9. Prioritize the 100 tactics according to resources.

10. Last, combine them all into a cohesive, unique marketing strategy for your company.

For a summary and step-by-step LinkedIn blog of the Fusion Marketing System, click here: http://linkd.in/1xveKlU]   And be sure to watch my **cartoon video** for more on the development of Fusion Marketing! You'll like it! video: http://bit.ly/1zGRRVl

Appendix A
The Deeper Approach

Appendix A
The Deeper Approach

In this appendix you will find the "Deeper Approach" that gives you a more specific, in-depth understanding of the concepts discussed above. We believe this will be the New Normal for how e-books are designed – practical summaries linked to more details for those who want them.

A link back to the relevant chapter have been provided at the end of each section here for your ease of use.

More on Our Research Methodology (see Chapter 2: Methods)

Based on Dr. Witt's experience in psychology and marketing research, and Lon Safko's knowledge of blogging, email, and Internet marketing, this is how we did our research.

- Analyzed each title for the presence of particular "hot button" words, presence of known motivating words, title length, presence of certain symbols, presence of numbers, complexity / simplicity of title, presence and clarity of any promise, type of concept in title, and focus on the reader.

- Compared results of top and bottom 25% (N=33) and top and bottom 33% (N=44) of titles on the factors noted above.

Determined percentage difference of specific words or ideas between top and bottom 25% and 33%. For example, if the word "hot" appeared 5 times in the bottom 25% of titles that were opened and 10 times in the top 25%, then you'd see the word "hot" showed a 100% increase for titles in the top 25%, suggesting it might be a good word to use in your own titles.

A positive number indicates higher usage of words as number of Views increases. A negative number (shown as <x>) indicates words that are more frequently used in low-view blog titles than in high-view blog titles, and generally should be avoided.

Selected for inclusion as guidelines only those factors which **exceeded a 33% difference** in both 25% and 33% category comparisons and had greater than 5 total blogs in both categories. Smaller data sets, such as 1 vs. 2, even though they may show a large percentage shift, are too small to be trusted. Nearly all factors included as Guidelines have far greater differences and number of blogs than these minimums. That is why the authors feel confident in the guidelines we are providing.

- Analyzed the types of lead picture that accompanied each blog title.

See Dave Kerpen's LinkedIn blog posts, including Views here: *http://linkd.in/1F17n14*

• • • • • • • • • • • • • • • • • • • •

Success, Successful, and Succeed (Chapter 3: Words)

The first rule of Marketing Psychology is that people do NOT want what you are selling, even if it is a free blog. They want to buy Satisfaction, whether that is the speed and hotness of a Corvette or the safety and room of a Volvo minivan. You might say that when clicking on a blog link they are not buying anything. But, they are spending their time, which is a cost to them.

Good advertising promises to sell them what they want. In this case, the titles promise Success. It might be in business, relationships, or how to dress. In any case, we all want to succeed in something. That is a satisfaction we all seek. Identify what that is for your target audience, then tack the word "Success" or "Successful" or "Succeed" into your title, and you have increased your chances of getting the targeted reader to open your blog by about 400% (according this is analysis).

• • • • • • • • • • • • • • • • • • • •

More on "Inspiring" Words (Chapter 3: Words)

As you'll see later, people want to not only improve their skills, but themselves as well. They want something that will take them out of the drudgery of their everyday work experience. Feeling inspired can be transformative, leading us in a direction where we feel happy, creative and excited. No wonder it is a powerful word to use in a "promise" title. It is also an emotional word. We often buy on the basis of emotion and justify it on the basis of logic, so <u>stimulating a desirable emotion</u> can be a great way to gain attention and action.

• •

More on Hot Words (Chapter 3: Words)

We like to think of ourselves as rational beings, but in truth there is an emotional component in almost every purchase we make. It pays to remember that if you are using your blogs to drive customers to your web site to sell them something. I'll point out two obvious gender-based examples: Women tend to lust after new shoes no matter how many are in the closet. Men tend to lust after sleek, fast cars no matter how impractical they are. Leaving the psychology of these responses aside, note that both are totally emotional responses to the sight of something desirable.

Our minds seek satisfaction of these desires. So if the shoes were $20 or the car was $2000, the value-to-price ratio of satisfying that desire would be so great that the money would be paid no matter how unneeded or impractical the objects are. Both genders do the same with lottery tickets. It has been calculated that the odds of winning the Powerball is about the same as your risk of being hit by lightning **28** times! Yet millions of people, knowing the odds are astronomical, still buy a cheap lottery ticket each week.

Logically they know they are throwing away their money. But, emotions are driving that train, the desire of winning "all that money!" And, that desire trumps logic every week. We cannot deny our emotions, no matter how loud logic shouted, "You don't need it!" Emotions simply reply, "Somebody's got to win!"

Brand _

memory sharing) _

The lesson, of course, is to make your product or service emotionally desirable so the buyer's decision is not just resting on logic. All the great brand names – Apple, Nike, Starbucks, Harley Davidson have powerful emotions associated with their brands -- emotions that buyers want to feel themselves, or make others believe about them. Emotions such as I'm cool, special, edgy not ordinary, smart, tough, etc. By buying the brand, they feel they are sending a message to everyone else about who they are, based on the image of the brand or product.

This is why you seldom see a man carrying a purse, no matter how convenient it might be. And why lots of women wear tops emblazoned with "Saks 5th Avenue," but you've never seen any woman wear a top proclaiming "I'm a K-Mart Woman!" We believe people judge us on what we wear, what we drive, what we drink, where we eat, and so on – because we know that we make that same judgement of others.

Probably the greatest example of this in advertising is the set of "attack positioning" ads called "Mac vs.

PC." Watch the entire series of these ads at http://bit.ly/1D4l25y.

In the Apple ads, if you like Apple, you are identifying with a character (and by extension the brand) who looks and dresses cool (well, cool for the target market), and shows a product that does cool things.

But, if you prefer the PC, then you see yourself being forced to identify with the PC character who is chubby and really nerdy in a brown suit and bad haircut, sounds clueless about the latest technology, and promotes a product that is behind the times (when asked about apps, he says "We have a calendar and a clock.")

Every spot pushes the watcher subconsciously to want to identify with Apple by promising they will feel cool and special with their cool and modern Apple computer. But, if they pick PC, the ad implies people will think they are dull nerds with a boring computer. That is how great emotional marketing is done, with subtlety and humor.

Watch the ads and apply their many lessons to your own advertising.

You can learn a lot about emotional marketing by studying ads like these. We all want to feel special. We try to do that in part by being identified with a special brand, one with a brand image we admire and believe our friends do, too, for example, Harley Davidson.. That is why you see women like to carry purses (even knock-offs) which proclaim a brand like Michael Kors, Gucci, or Louis Vuitton. But have you ever seen a Sears brand purse?

Back to Your Place

• • • • • • • • • • • • • • • • • • • •

More on "How To" Chapter 3: Words)

The phrase "How To" is different from simply using the word "How," which showed no difference in response between top and bottom titles. A sentence starting with "How" can go in many directions, like "How Crowdemand is Disrupting Fashion" which pulled only 8,900 Views.) http://linkd.in/1AbGjsX.

But, "How To" promises you will learn how to do something. This promise offers two important satisfactions. The new skill can save us money/time/frustration, and it can make us feel more confident about ourselves, our ability to do what needs to be done without asking for help. For example, "How To Dress for Success

Today" pulled 345,000 Views. (http://linkd.in/1tBwflC).

Remember, using "How To" improves your odds tremendously for a View, but it is not foolproof. Success also depends on the skill paired with it. For example "How Successful People Think" offered a valuable skill for 133,000 people, (http://linkd.in/1tJ6JRI), while "How To Ward Off Time *Vampires*" (http://linkd.in/1xlesNE), only seemed valuable to 13,000 people, not surprising given the title. Make sure your promised skill is both highly desirable and expressed simply, as a clear promise.

• • • • • • • • • • • • • • • • • • • •

More on "Never" (Chapter 3: Words)

Most people are risk-adverse in their careers, preferring to take fewer chances rather than risk losing. When we are offered a tip which can help us avoid risks, we are interested, such as "Never Make This Investing Mistake." The word "Never" sends up an emotional red flare fear from our subconscious mind that we ought to know whatever information is behind the title so we will never do it if we're in that situation, such as "The One Thing Never To Do If You Smell Gas!" Note how the use of an exclamation mark heightens the warning of danger.

You'll note that this is far different from "Always" (which is not used in Dave's titles). "Always" suggests actions we should take. "Always look both ways before crossing the street" and "Always wash your hands after using the bathroom" are good rules, but sometimes we don't follow them. They don't have the fear the power of "Never"; they just offer good advice. And, since almost every blog offers good advice of some sort, "Always" doesn't have the emotional impact to set its title apart from all the others.

• •

More on "Secret" (Chapter 3: Words)

People want to know what others do not. That is the underlying power of gossip. We'll gossip about co-workers, snoop in the medicine cabinet of our party host, or sneak a peek at a handwritten letter sent to our spouse, all to satisfy our curiosity. Partly this is genetic. One laboratory study on curiosity gave caged monkeys the choice between looking out a window and eating. Until they got really hungry, monkeys would choose the visual stimulation outside the window over food.

Advertisers use this. For example, an ad in which the headline is handwritten, especially on a piece of letter paper, is more effective than the same headline printed in a common font at the top of the page. When the copy is written as a letter to someone ("Dear Beth...") or a message from someone, it pulls better than the same copy in a standard ad format. We like to read other people's mail!

This is usually just an emotional behavior. We have no logical reason to satisfy our curiosity. It is more like an itch that we want to scratch, like the old saying about the cat.

Remember that as you design your ads, your copy or your headlines. As an example, one of Dave's best-performing headlines is "The One Thing You Must Do in Every Job Interview"(http://linkd.in/1Dlgrtf), which garnered 706,000 Views.

What percentage of his readers do you think were actually looking for a job or expected to be? I'll bet there were a lot more readers who thought they might benefit by reading his "11 Simple Secrets to Handling e-Mails on Vacation," (http://linkd.in/13RbYll). But, that blog had under 12,000 readers, while "The One Thing You Must Absolutely, Always Say in an Interview" pulled 706,000 readers! I don't know about you, but I'd still like to know that one thing I should do! Curiosity is a driving force in human beings. Use it to your advantage in your headlines and blog copy.

• • • • • • • • • • • • • • • • • • • •

More on the Blog Opening (Chapter 3: Words)

Generating a blog View is generally a two-step process: First, the reader looks at the picture if one is present, then the title. The 1.5 Second Rule© comes into play here, create immediate interest. Second, if it creates interest, the reader looks at the opening sentence or two below the title. In some cases, the title itself is so appealing that readers just click it without looking ("Free Starbucks Today!") If the title hasn't completely compelled readers to commit, they may glance at the opening sentences in hopes of more appeal.

While the title does the heavy lifting, the introductory sentences need to reinforce the appeal created by the title. In the example above about Starbucks, the opening sentence might read *"All Grandes Free today only – customer appreciation giveaway!"*

The sentence does several important things. It uses the most powerful of all marketing words, "Free," explains when and where, and provides a reason for the generosity to reduce the reader's fear of a scam. We desire the freebie, but our logical brain needs to be quieted after it shouts, "Why should they give it away?" The answer doesn't have to be great, just enough to provide a reason that sounds logical. When logic is competing with emotion, it is already fighting with one hand tied behind its back!

You'll notice the Starbucks' sentence reinforces the title's promise, stimulates an emotion, provides clarification, and reduces fear. Together these elements make the reader more likely to want to view the blog. Just a reminder – the opening sentence or two is the blurb people read under your blog title, so it must do heavy duty marketing for the blog.

Finally, you can use the words and other elements identified in this book in your opening sentences as well as your title. Sometimes we can hit two powerful but separate notes that way.

For example, "11 Simple Solutions to Remove Any Stain" is a pretty good positive promise title. Follow that with an opening sentence of "Get rid of all stains and never make this terrible mistake!" This is followed by a quick fear story about someone who made a big, foolish mistake when trying to get a stain out – when the right answer was in this book! In this way, the blogger offers a benefit and creates a fear at the same time (notice the use of the word 'never' in the title to create fear and curiosity?) Opening the blog gives them two practical pieces of information for free.

• •

More About Numbers (Chapter 3: Words)

Many bloggers and advertisers recognize that numbers are a powerful way of attracting readers. We like numbers for their specificity and because they seem to offer "bite-sized" chunks of information – we can read a few then skip around to others without losing anything.

Numbers are nearly always followed by some noun, like Tips, Rules, Guidelines, Mistakes, etc. The clear promise is that each one will provide a stand-alone piece of information that readers will be able to apply as soon as they wish.

This e-book is written in what we're calling the *New Normal* of writing style, lots of bullet points and short paragraphs, basics and facts, links to more information if desired, including videos, but removed from the main body of the book so as to not impede the skimming preference of today's reader. Successful blogs, which offer short, simple, easy to digest tidbits of information are often in this preferred format. Titles which promise such small, numbered confections are more likely to be opened, read, liked, and shared.

• • • • • • • • • • • • • • • • • • •

More on Odd-Even Numbers (Chapter 4: Numbers)

We looked at this odd/even difference and found that Dave used 26 odd numbers (excluding 1, which was not counted since people equate numbers with a list of multiple numbers, which is more than one), but only 6 even numbers.

Two key facts stood out: First, the top 33% of titles contained over twice as many numbers as the bottom 33%. Numbers clearly influenced the click rate. Second, of the six even numbers used, 5 appeared in the top 33%, only one at the bottom. In other words, even numbers performed better – 5:1 versus 2:1 for the odd numbers! Consider the small data sample of number of even numbers before jumping to conclusions. In any case, you can use even numbers without concern, they may even perform better.

• • • • • • • • • • • • • • • • • • •

More on Number Size (Chapter 4: Numbers)

Twenty titles used number 2 - 10. The lower half (numbers 2 – 5) had a 4 to 3 split when comparing the top to bottom third of the titles. The upper half (numbers 6 – 10) had over twice as many titles at the top than at the bottom, 9 to 4. What this means is that larger lists don't seem to stop readers from clicking.

13 titles used numbers above 10, double digit-numbers. Of those, 9 appeared in the top third. That gives double-digit numbers a 69% chance of appearing at the top, whereas single digit numbers have a 65% appearance rate. The percentages are so close, there's no reasonable difference between using single or double-digit numbers; both are powerful. Again, despite logic to the contrary, the size of Dave's lists didn't affect the number of Views. So use any number you want without too much concern.

• •

More on Questions (Chapter 4: Numbers)

We strongly suspect that most of the poor results of question marks are due to the poor questions they posed in Dave's blogs. Here are the question titles in the bottom 33%. See if you agree they don't hold much interest to most readers.

• Can Women Put an End to Sexist Politics? (http://linkd.in/1xHCwTV)

- Can the #ALSIceBucketChallenge be Repeated? (http://linkd.in/1D7vTf4)
- Should You Take a Summer Vacation? (http://linkd.in/1Kctulf)
- What's Missing from an Entrepreneur's Life? (http://linkd.in/1rUdwpZ)
- How Important Is Luck in Success? (http://linkd.in/1w5OOzu)
- Genius or Total Sellout? Creativity for Sale (http://linkd.in/1AtrWPF)
- More Important to Success: Hard Work or Luck? (http://linkd.in/1rUe2Ei)

An 8th title asked a question without including a question mark, "What color is your Parachute" (http://linkd.in/1KctRfG).

None of these titles seems particularly appealing to a wide audience, and often lack any specific promise or stated value for the majority of readers. They also are missing other words we've identified as valuable in getting Views. No wonder these titles averaged just 13,200 readers.

A study of 150,000 article headlines done by Outbrain.com in 2011 (referenced by Content Marketing Institute) found that titles with question marks had a higher click-through rate than those ending in an exclamation mark or a period. Many advertisers, including the famed David Ogilvy, believe that questions create strong headlines. He also said that exclamation marks (!) create a stronger headline. Ogilvy did a study which found putting a period at the end of a headline increased the ad's recall rate. In part, he attributed this to the period making the title look different from other ad titles – and "different" helps ads stand out.

**More on Promises and Marketing Psychology
(Chapter 5: Promises)**

Clearly your promise must interest the reader.
That's why the first commandment of marketing is
"Know Thy Customer." Too often marketers equate
"knowing" customers with their demographic data;
age, sex, education, income, etc. If that's all you
know, you have no idea what to promise them. You
know external information, but your customers live
INSIDE their heads and that's what you need to
understand.

To understand more about marketing psychology,
click here to hear a story by Dr. Witt.

In Marketing Psychology, we look at four basic areas
in a Buyer Motivation Analysis (BMA). Each
segment of your target market must have its own
BMA. Why? Because each segment or even micro

segment has its own unique buying motivations, its own particular satisfactions. This becomes obvious if you ask yourself if you would use the same ad to sell blue jeans to an 18-year-old girl and a 65-year-old woman?

While there's a great deal to creating professional customer research and data analysis, you can give yourself an edge over competitors just by doing some introspective analysis of your customers, or just having a chat with some of them.

Here's how: Customers buy based on logic and emotion, and often will buy primarily on emotion and justify it to themselves and others with logic. I'll mention just two categories as gender-based examples; shoes and Corvettes. Both are often purchased on the basis of emotion, but justified by the most tenuous logic.

Why? Because we like to think of ourselves as logical, not swayed. So we need a "logic" peg on which to hang our emotion, like a beautiful but impractical ball gown hung up on a plain wire coat hanger. The star, the dress, needs the help of the plain coat hanger in order to shine. We need some logical reason, however tenuous, to support our emotional choice.

Make sure you provide some logical appeal in your "fear" or "desire" based messages to hang your emotional messages on. Your readers need it.

Both logical and emotional motivators can be missed by your research unless you are doing a careful BMA to uncover them. It is important that you do. If you can identify these hidden motivators, you can tailor your headlines, picture, and blog copy to satisfy them. Use the following four categories of the BMA to provide your answer. This is best done with careful research, but even a half hour of introspection and visiting with customers will provide some helpful ideas.

You'll read about the four types of motivators below. If you would like to hear Dr. Witt explain more about marketing psychology,

NEEDS

Needs is a logical motivator. These are things we believe we must have in order to satisfy a problem. If our growing family requires little Johnny to ride in the trunk of the family car, the satisfaction we need is to transport our large family in safety and comfort. We don't need a particular car or SUV, anything that will do the job satisfies the need. Any SUV will work, but a Miata won't. Needs are deal-breakers. If you can't get close to these satisfactions, you won't buy.

We'll normally have several needs related to the product category, like capacity, total price, operating cost, etc. But, one or two will be the key factors. Those are the ones to emphasize in your marketing materials. For example, the soccer mom segment rates safety as the most important benefit needed in a vehicle for obvious reasons. A headline like "Hit 60 MPH in 5 Seconds!" does not ring the right bell with the soccer mom segment. "Highest Family Protection Rating" does ring the right bell for her. Needs tell you the right bell to ring in the headline, picture, and body copy. You'll have others, but that one leads!

WANTS

Wants is a logical motivator. Wants are not deal-breakers like Needs are. If the soccer mom wants an SUV in white, because she thinks it looks classier (and thus makes her look classier), but can save money with a red one, she may take it. There will be quite a few Wants in your list. Some may appear on both lists. For example, in a household cleaner, "No stinky smell" may be a Need, but a "Pleasant Smell" could be a Want.

Identify a few top Wants and use them in the body copy of your blog or ad. They support your pitch, but are not the leading actors. They are often the tipping point that gives you the nod over a competitor. If the SUVs of two dealers are the same in style and price, but if one dealer offers a free oil change for 3 years, satisfying that small Want can tip the deal in his favor.

FEARS

Fear is an emotional motivator. **Fears are the marketer's greatest friend.** We buy billions of dollars of products and services every year on the basis of fear, from life insurance to deodorant to shampoos that promise to rid us of dandruff so we won't be embarrassed by it. If you can make buyers believe they will avoid embarrassment by buying your product, you can back your armored car up to the bank.

For example, advertising for Wisk laundry detergent made wives believe the faint discoloration around the inside of their husbands' white shirt collars was a source of secret scorn by others, making her feel embarrassed and then determined to solve that imaginary problem – enter new Wisk!

You'll find that your list of Fears is tied closely to Needs. Our soccer moms NEED a safe vehicle because they FEAR their children could be hurt in an accident. Like needs, your top fear is a leading character in your marketing message, including your blog headline and picture. One of the greatest ads of all time showed a picture of a destitute young Depression era family, mother and two small children, over the headline *"He Didn't Have Life Insurance."* The ad was for New York Life Insurance.

Good fear-based pictures and headlines must <u>first</u> create a Big Fear; then promise to take it away. Only then do you use your features to prove you can deliver on that promise. That's what the reader wants at that moment, and why they will "act now" if you do the ad correctly following this three step approach – create Fear, promise to remove it with your product or service, prove you can deliver by emphasizing your best features. That is the correct order – NOT starting with your features!

DESIRES

Desires is an emotional motivator category. Desires are daydreams. We don't expect them to come true, but because they are emotional and thus immune to logic, we still hold them with hope that they might.

Millions repeatedly buy diet pills from television ads despite knowing they likely won't work and can be dangerous. The same is true for all those weird pieces of exercise equipment that don't work. Our desire to look attractive is so great we will ban logic from our decision.

Marketers can use key Desire motivators as leading actors. Usually there will be only a couple of identifiable desires. If you have more than a few on your list, chances are you really listed Wants. If your Desires and Fears are not clearly EMOTIONS, they don't belong on these lists. The two most common types of desires are related to self-image, and the way others see us, which, of course, then feeds back to our self-image.

We desire others to love us, to respect us and to believe we are special or admirable in some way, such as being cool, sexy, smart, powerful, etc. We desire to see ourselves as the hero, the great caregiver, the adventurer, the wise person, the accomplished person, the "go to" person. We desire to feel pride in what we have done. Smart marketers promise we can have what we desire -- with the help of their product. We also desire to have others think well of us when we've done something admirable. Done a good job cleaning the kitchen? Advertisers will show you and your kitchen being admired by your best friend, your husband (unlikely!) or even your mother-in-law (jackpot!). *[handwritten annotation]*

Sex is the most common type of desire ad themes. The premise is that the target market reading / viewing the ad wants more sex, or to attract desirable partners to have sex with. So, show the person what they desire, a sexual situation they can project themselves into. It is the sex equivalent to the wedding couple seen in the eHarmony ad above.

Now that you have stimulated their desire, the next step is to promise to satisfy it with your product. This really is a simple layout – big picture of attractive people making out and a smaller picture of your product, which could be a variety of things from perfume to wine to diamonds, maybe even a good steak or a fur coat. It doesn't matter.

The implication by pairing two things together, the couple and the product, that the viewer makes the connection – if I want this, I need to buy that. There is no logic to it at all, but it doesn't matter. Desires and fears are not driven by logic, but by emotion.

We are all subconsciously susceptible to our desires. Otherwise no one would buy lottery tickets! In your marketing message, just remember to begin with the desires, reminding people of how nice it would be, then bring in the product to save the day, and close with the praise and back-patting buyers dream about. Logical? No. Works? Yes!

Want to understand more about how to use Marketing Psychology in your marketing strategy. Listen to Dr. Witt's story about the Giant Rat of Sumatra and how you can translate motivations into concrete marketing messages that work

• • • • • • • • • • • • • • • • • • • •

More on Dave's Photos (Chapter 6: Photos)

The results of this 132 blog / image sample are so far off what we know about photos that we are nearly certain most of the pictures didn't help or hurt readership at all. In other words, leave out the pictures and the Views would likely have been about

the same. People went on to look at the headline –
likely because Dave's reputation led them to move
past the picture, which then drew them into many of
the blogs. If you don't have Dave's reputation, then
you need all the help you can get, and that means
good pictures.

Dave's images, most of which are illustrative and
generic, can be broken down into four categories by
content;
1) Images of Words,
2) Images of Things,
3) Images with Multiple People, and
4) Images with close-ups of one or two people.

Within the last category, we also tallied those in
which the people were looking out at the reader.
Other research clearly shows a close-up with the
model looking directly out at the reader has great

stopping power, that is why it's the standard in most professional ads.

Dave's results are exactly backward from what should be the case. A close-up of a person looking at the reader draws far better than an image of a word, but here the word image draws 300% better.

After analysis, we suggest that very few of the images were performing as images should: grabbing attention and making a visual promise. Most readers likely glanced at them, gained nothing, then looked over at the title, which did the real work of getting Views.

• • • • • • • • • • • • • • • • • • • •

More on the Psychology of Good Advertising Pictures (Chapter 6: Photos)

The following is taken from Dr. Witt's book *High Impact: How You Can Create Advertising That Sells!*

"Selecting the right type of picture for your blog can attract more readers. The following techniques for selecting pictures are founded on the results of psychological and advertising research, practical experience and the physiology of human vision. Here are just a few examples of how to pick a picture.

1. Use Startling Pictures.

A picture with a startling image will attract a lot of attention. A picture of a cow in a tree is an example. Coupled with a headline like, "How To Avoid an Ill Wind in Your Life," and you've got the structure which will lead readers right into your blog. This ad with a startled baby ties nicely into the title, which also uses the high-attraction word "startling" to tease the reader into wanting to know more.

2. Use People

People love to look at other people. The people in your photo should be doing something interesting, puzzling, or fun, rather than just standing around like they're waiting for a bus, unless they are gorgeous models showing off some product. Often beauty is enough. In general though, people in action are just more interesting to look at. Crowd shots without a clear focus don't often work. They don't offer any arresting subject for the eye to focus on. Especially for smaller pictures normally used with blogs, a photo of a single person is usually better, and a close-up is best.

3. Use Tight Close-ups of People Looking Directly at the Reader

There are few pictures that will draw more attention than a close up of a person staring with both eyes at the reader, not off camera or down, but directly at the reader. When people look at us, even in a picture, we tend to look at them. That captures attention. But, you need more. A second element must create curiosity or a promise leading the reader to click your link. For example, this picture works with a headline like "Are Your Eyebrows Too Long?"

4. Use Humorous Images

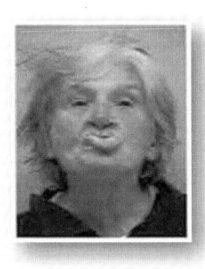

Photos which are immediately funny can be attractive. Baby animals at play have great potential for providing such scenes. So do photos which look at a common object in a funny, novel way, such as a little boy on his knees trying to push a bowling ball down the alley, or this one of a woman sticking her tongue out. Tie it to a grabber headline like "Would Your Mom Hate Your Customer Service?" and you've got a strong lure for readers.

5. Place a Common Object in an Uncommon Setting

A little girl standing on a playground may not be eye-catching, but a little girl in her play clothes standing on an automobile assembly line, or in the middle of a road, or on the floor of the New York Stock Exchange will grab viewers' attention. A car parked on the street is boring, but the same car parked in a church isn't. We expect people and things to be found in a range of settings which are common for them, such as a playground or school for the little girl.

When the setting is far outside the normal range of what we expect, the picture doesn't make immediate sense, so we stop to investigate because it has aroused our curiosity. Pair it with a great headline and you get a click!

6. Make the Object Big

A close-up photo can often grab attention, especially if it is of a familiar object. Small or even tiny objects seem to work especially well. A tight close-up of an apple or a grape, the veins in a leaf, or a caterpillar are all good examples. This picture shows an eye in an arresting way. Paired with a headline like "Everyone Will Watch You." it will interest and attract readers.

7. Show Them Their Desires

We all need and want things, and we all fear certain outcomes. But, in our heart of hearts, we daydream about our desires. The movie star we want to kiss, the job that would make our career fly, the little house on a quiet beach, these images are so strong sometimes you can almost touch them.

Images of our daydreams are powerful motivators. For example, you could pair this photo with the headline, "You CAN Make This Your New Office!" **The general rule in marketing psychology is to first stimulate a desire, then promise to satisfy it.** The picture raises the desire; the headline promises to deliver it.

These are only a few of the picture tips found in Dr. Witt's *High Impact*, along with dozens of guidelines on headlines, body copy, layout, and brand image positioning.

● ●

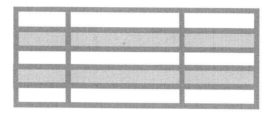

Appendix B

Tables

Appendix B
Tables

The following tables mathematically summarize our findings in the text. For those of you so inclined, you can study the actual differences and draw your own conclusions. Keep in mind that small differences are likely not significant because they are based on such a small sample size. That is why we only focused on those which are so large they are worth analyzing.

Table 1
Analysis of Key Words in Top and Bottom 25% and 33% of Blog Title Views.

Word or Phrase	Number of Those Words in Top & Bottom 25%		% Change in Views:	Number of Words in Top & Bottom 33%		% Change in Views:
	Top (N=33)	Botto m (N=33)	Top vs Botto m 25%	Top (N= 44)	Bot to m (N= 44)	Top vs Botto m 33%
Job/Ca reer	1	0	n.s.	2	1	100%
Leader	3	2	50%	3	3	nc
Why/W hat	1	3	<66%>	2	3	<33%>
Secret	4	3	33%	4	4	nc
Succes s, etc.	5	1	400%	5	2	150%
You/Yo urs	10	5	100%	13	11	18%
Simple	2	3	<33%>	3	3	nc
How	2	2	nc	2	2	nc
How To	2	2	nc	4	2	100%
Lesson s/Tips	2	1	100%	2	2	nc
Best/M ost	3	2	50%	3	3	nc
Never	2	0	n.s.	2	0	n.s.
Inspire, etc.	4	1	300%	4	1	300%
Hot Words* *	15	10	50%	20	13	54%

Note: "Etc." indicates all words with same base were counted, like "success" and "successful." "nc" shows no change across cells. "n.s." means no statistical analysis possible due to denominator being a zero. Realistically, though, moving from nothing to a high word usage is a significant finding. You'll see good examples of this in Table 2 just below.

** *Hot words* are those which provoke interest or desire in the reader. They include: simple, secret, profit, profitable, win, inspire, incredible, opportunity, future, trends, accomplish, weird, scary, F-word, success, succeed, power, new, dream, independence, amazing, happiness, Lady Gaga, destroy, strength. Several of these have also been evaluated separately due to their prevalent use.

Factors which show at least a 33% difference in both 25% and 33% categories are highlighted in Yellow. Factors which show a negative 33% difference in both 25% and 33% categories are highlighted in Orange.

Back to My Place

• •

Table 2
Analysis of Symbols and Numbers in Top and Bottom 25% and 33% of Blog Title Views.

Symbol or Number	How Many Used in Top & Bottom 25%		% Change in Views: Top vs Bottom 25%	How Many Used in Top & Bottom 33%		% Change in Views: Top vs Bottom 33%
	Top	Bottom		Top	Bottom	
Colon (:)	0	8	0.5	1	12	<92%>
Question Mark (?)	0	6	0.5	1	8	<88%>
Number > 1 (indicating a list in text)	17	8	113%	22	11	100%

• •

Table 3
Analysis of Types of Promises Made in Headlines

Headline contains ...	How Many Used in Top & Bottom 25%		Change in Top vs Bottom	How Many Used in Top & Bottom 33%		Change in Top vs Bottom
	Top	Bottom		Top	Bottom	
Clear, simple promise	9	5	80%	13	6	117%
6 or fewer words in title	6	11	<45%>	10	11	<9%>
Concept of improving yourself	23	10	130%	29	13	123%

• •

Table 4

Analysis of Positive Versus Negative Key Words in Top and Bottom 25% and 33% of Blog Title Views

Type of Key Words	Number of Key Words in Top & Bottom 25%		Change in Bottom to Top 25% of Views	Number of Key Words in Top & Bottom 33%		Change in Bottom to Top 33% of Views
	Top	Bottom		Top	Bottom	
Positive Key Words*	45	20	125%	58	27	115%
Negative Key Words*	2	9	<78%>	4	15	<73%>

• •

Table 5

Analysis of Type of Picture Attached to Blog Title

Type of Picture	Number of Pictures in Top & Bottom 33%		Ratio of Top Rated to Bottom Rated Blogs Using These Types of Pictures
	Top☐33%	Bottom☐33%	
Words	7	3	2.3 :1
Things	11	8	1.4 :1
Multiple People	15	13	1.15 :1
CU shot of 1-2 persons	11	20	0.55 :1

Decades of research on images confirms that pictures of people, especially close up photos, have higher rates of attention than landscapes, abstracts, or words. Yet this analysis shows just the opposite. The only conclusion is that the pictures were of no importance in the reader's decision to view Dave's blog. We suspect that Dave's fame has a lot to do with this finding. Dave's trust factor is so high that his readers will look at the blog title no matter what the picture beside it is.

* *

Appendix C
Resource Materials

Resources

Lon Safko
The Social Media Bible

Hit #1 on Amazon!
The bestselling bible for social media is now completely revised and updated!
The Social Media Bible, Third Edition
(www.TheSocialMediaBible.com)
is the most comprehensive

resource now in five languages, that transforms the way corporate, small business, and non-profit companies use social media to reach their desired audiences with power messages and efficiency. In this Third Edition, each of the three parts – Tactics, Tools, and Strategies – have been updated to reflect the most current social media trends.

The Social Media Bible covers all major new software applications, including features and benefits, in detail. Lists more than 120 companies integral to the social media industry with updated data, products, services, and links. Includes advanced topics like measuring social media return on investment (ROI) and how to develop and implement the Five Steps to Social Media Success strategy plan and includes dozens of social media ROI case studies.

The   Social   Media   Bible,
(www.TheSocialMediaBible.com) Third Edition gives you a fully up-to-date toolbox to revamp your marketing strategy and create new opportunities for growth.

Praise for *The Social Media Bible:*

"The social media phenomenon is still ramping up and this book provides useful and timely business advice."
Vint Cerf, Father Of The Internet

"Lon is a serial technologist who really understands social media and is also blessed with the gift of being a great communicator. His book deftly takes you from "Social Media 101" all the way to PhD status in a format that is easy to browse, informative and powerful."
Tom Asher, Director Consumer Relations North America, Levi Strauss & Co

"Lon Safko and The Social Media Bible address the key questions – Why should I take part in Social Media? How should I take part? How do I reap the greatest benefits? – while also providing the push to take the next step."
Jeff Hagen, Director, Consumer Services, General Mills

"Effectively harnessing the power of social media is a top priority in corporate America. "The Social Media Bible" with its informative and tactical approach, provides an easy-to-follow roadmap for how to do social media right."
Todd Simon, Senior Vice President, Omaha Steaks

"Social Media and Customer Care are rapidly coming together. This Edition is a must read for any professional who wants to stay on top of this rapidly changing topic. From the basics to long term Social

Media strategy, this is the only resource book to have on your desk."
Scott Ross, Senior Vice President, Sales & Marketing, NCO Group

Order here: http://amzn.to/1wDaGb0

● ●

The Fusion Marketing Bible, It's What's Next!

Hit   #3   on   Amazon!

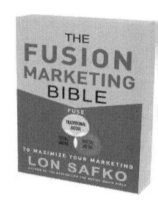

(http://www.TheFusionMarketingBible.com)

If you are still calling yourself a "Social Media Expert" then you're announcing to the world that you have been left behind. If you're an expert in Facebook or Twitter, then you're trying to build your marketing restricted to using only two tools. Social media is an amazing marketing tool set, take it from me, I wrote the book on it (the best selling The Social Media Bible)! If you're still stuck looking at social media as a stand alone technology, then you've been left behind.

The   Fusion   Marketing   Bible (http://www.TheFusionMarketingBible.com) is the next step that brings our 6,000 years of traditional marketing, the exciting digital marketing tools of the

Internet, and social media and fully integrates them into one seamless tool set that will accomplish every goal you set!

The Fusion Marketing Bible isn't just about integration; it's about a totally new concept of "Interconnecting" all of your traditional, digital, and social media tools. *The Fusion Marketing Bible* is about looking at all of your tools, campaigns, and conversion strategies first in two-dimensions, then taking all of your marketing strategies into the world of three-dimensions. 3D allows you to look at everything you do in marketing in a completely different way! And, it's Patent Pending!

Order here: http://amzn.to/16aWR83

* *

Dr. Gary Witt
High Impact: How to Create Ads That Sell!

You should own this book if you have a small business, home-based business, e-commerce business, create print ads or brochures, or want your print advertising to bring in more customers. This is the cheapest way to make more sales you'll ever find! Guaranteed.

Over 500 tips, ideas and "how-to" guidelines show you step-by-step how to create powerful, effective ads, brochures and flyers. Anyone can use these tips to help their business grow.

You can be using its proven ideas within hours -- open, look, think, and apply. No long days of study! Stop missing sales with your mediocre advertising! Fix it NOW. A better ad is the cheapest and most effective way to improve your advertising ROI!

PRAISE FOR HIGH IMPACT: "If Madison Avenue creatives understood half of what you are saying, their advertising would improve tenfold!" -- Richard Potter, Power Advertising, Los Angeles

Why Should You Own This eBook Today?

*   Designed for business people who know little or nothing about advertising.
*   A detailed, step-by-step plan to make all your advertising and marketing more effective.

- Easy-to-read, simple-to-apply ideas. Find what you need, and how to do it quickly.
- Saves you time and money starting now.
- Own a reference work you'll use year after year.
- Easy to understand tips and techniques make ads really pay off in higher ROI.
- Analyze your current advertising, and your competitors', for weaknesses.
- You have a 100% MONEY BACK GUARANTEE of satisfaction!

Order   Here: www.marketingpsychology.com/Resources.

Read an excerpt and you'll be convinced you need this book!

Dave Kerpen
Likeable Social Media

The New York Times And USA Today Bestseller!

The secret to successful word-of-mouth marketing on the social web is easy: BE LIKEABLE.

A friend's recommendation is more powerful than any advertisement. In the world of Facebook, Twitter, and beyond, that recommendation can travel farther and faster than ever before.

Likeable Social Media helps you harness the power of word-of-mouth marketing to transform your business. Listen to your customers and prospects. Deliver value, excitement, and surprise. And, most important, learn how to truly engage your customers and help them spread the word.

Praise for *Likeable Social Media*:
"Dave Kerpen's insights and clear, how-to instructions on building brand popularity by truly engaging with customers on Facebook, Twitter, and the many other social media platforms are nothing short of brilliant."
Jim McCann, founder of 1-800-FLOWERS.COM and Celebrations.com

"Alas, common sense is not so common. Dave takes you on a (sadly, much needed) guided tour of how to

be human in a digital world."
Seth Godin, author of *Poke the Box*

"Likeable Social Media cuts through the marketing jargon and technical detail to give you what you really need to make sense of this rapidly changing world of digital marketing and communications. Being human — being likeable — will get you far."
Scott Monty, Global Digital Communications, Ford Motor Company

"Dave gives you what you need: Practical, specific how-to advice to get people talking about you."
Andy Sernovitz, author of *Word of Mouth Marketing: How Smart Companies Get People Talking*

Order Here: http://amzn.to/1vYDXY1

* * * * * * * * * * * * * * * * * * * *

139

Recommended Reading

Likeable Business: Why Today's Consumers Demand More and How Leaders Can Deliver
Dave Kerpen

ht tp://amzn.to/1Faq5P9

Socialnomics: How Social Media Transforms the Way We Live and Do Business
Erik Qualman

ht tp://amzn.to/1xxucnY

What Happens in Vegas Stays on YouTube
Erik Qualman

ht tp://amzn.to/1tK0A7k

Facebook Marketing All-in-One For Dummies
Andrea Vahl

h ttp://amzn.to/1ApcuTl

Go Mobile: Location-Based Marketing, Apps, Mobile Optimized Ad Campaigns, 2D Codes and Other Mobile Strategies to Grow Your Business

Jamie
Tuner

ttp://amzn.to/1KeSFnt <u>h</u>

How to Make Money with Social Media: An Insider's Guide on Using New and Emerging Media to Grow Your Business

Turner

Jamie

tp://amzn.to/1BBgUX1 <u>ht</u>

The Third Screen, New Edition: The Ultimate Guide to Mobile Marketing

Martin

Chuck

tp://amzn.to/1xKMiok <u>ht</u>

Mobile Influence: The New Power of the Consumer

Martin

Chuck

tp://amzn.to/1xKZBSt <u>ht</u>

Social Media Marketing eLearning Kit for Dummies

Khare

Phyllis

ht tp://bit.ly/1AT4ywt

LinkedIn Marketing: An Hour a Day Viveka von

Rosen

ht tp://amzn.to/1vUENnF

Appendix D

Author Biographies

Biographies

Dr. Gary Witt

Dr. Gary Witt is an award-winning professor of marketing, communication and psychology at seven different universities, and has also lectured in Rome. He consults with businesses and associations in buyer persuasion through his Marketing Psychology company. He holds a doctorate in both psychology and communication from the University of Texas, plus 20 years of marketing experience focused on the behavior and persuasion of buyers.

Dr. Witt's Marketing Psychology clients have included USWest Telephone, Kodak, Western Dental, the largest dental chain in California, MultiPlan PPOs New York, Allied Global Partners (Tokyo), and Harrah's, among many others. His work for clients includes an in-depth proprietary Buyer Motivation Analysis (BMA) to uncover deeper psychological buying triggers, and detailed guidance in applying the results to create marketing strategies and messages.

This BMA analysis creates a solid customer psychology platform on which all marketing decisions can be made with more certainty.

Dr. Witt is the creator of the multi-award-winning "*Newscast From The Past*" PBS television series, and executive producer of its "*Timeline*" series. He has also been a TV anchorman, News Director, documentary producer, lobbyist, PR director, radio DJ, and Communication Director.

144

Dr. Witt has written a book on marketing and advertising, *High Impact: How You Can Create Ads That Sell!*, and *101 Ways to Improve Your Business Website*, as well as a college textbook on developmental psychology. *His 73-Point Website Marketing Strength Inventory* has helped many improve the marketing power of their website. He is writing a book on the application of European marketing methods for American businesses. He lives in Scottsdale, AZ with his wife, who writes books for new parents.

Contact Gary at: witt@marketingpsychology.com, or 480-223-7705

Back to Introduction

Biographies

Lon Safko

Lon Safko is a bestselling author, speaker, trainer, consultant, and is the creator of the "First Computer To Save A Human Life" as coined by Steve Jobs, Apple, Inc. That computer, along with 18 other inventions and more than 30,000 of Lon's papers, are in the Smithsonian Institution in Washington, D.C. This alone is a testimony to Lon's creativity.

Lon is the host of the world's first PBS Television Special "*Social Media & You... Communicating in a Digital World*".

Lon went on to create numerous hardware and software solutions for the physically challenged, developed the first CAD software for civil engineers, designed the archetypes for the Apple Newton & Microsoft's Bob Operating Systems, and is also responsible for those handy little Tool-Tips help-balloon pop-ups!

Lon has founded over 14 successful companies, including Paper Models, Inc., which developed Three-Dimensional Internet Advertising and Virtual-Electronic-Retailing "V-E-Tailing" for business, promotions, and education for which Lon holds three United States Patents.

Lon has been recognized for his creativity with such prestigious awards as: The Westinghouse Entrepreneur of the Year, Arizona Innovation Network's Innovator of the Year, The Arizona Software Association's Entrepreneur of the Year, twice nominated for the Ernst & Young / Inc. Magazine Entrepreneur of the Year, The Public Relations Society of America's, Edward Bernay's, Mark of Excellence Award, and nominated as a Fellow to the nation's Computer History Museum. Lon has also been featured in Entrepreneur Magazine, PC Novice, INC. Magazine, CFO, Popular Science Magazines and the New York Times just to name a few. Lon was even selected by the Smithsonian Institution to represent "The American Inventor" at their annual conference, and is now part of the Guinness World Records!

Lon is an author of remarkable breadth, writing nine innovative bestselling books, which have helped guide corporations in mastering social media marketing, integrating traditional, digital, and social media marketing. Lon trains executives to think creatively, uncovering the secrets of increasing customers, sales and revenue.

Lon's bestselling book published by John Wiley & Sons *The Social Media Bible* unlocks the mysteries of the hottest new Internet wave, Social Media, such as Facebook, Twitter, and LinkedIn, for business. This book is transforming corporate, government, and non-profit marketing strategies and how they use these new media to reach their desired audiences with powerful messages and efficiency. His book hit #1 on Amazon in both Business & Marketing categories, is in its Third Edition and five languages. Lon is also a professional blogger for Fast Company, appointed the first Ambassador to SCORE, and is a USAToday CEO Advisor.

Lon's newest bestseller *The Fusion Marketing Bible*, published by McGraw Hill will truly change the way we do marketing and sales by looking at marketing in a completely different way; 3D! Along with Lon's other inventions, The Safko Wheel Marketing Toolkit, concept will leverage your existing marketing to make it significantly more effective, while adding to your company's bottom-line without any additional expense!

Lon is in high demand as a speaker literally around the world, giving keynote addresses and private C-Suite workshops from Rome and Vienna to Singapore, Mumbai and Dubai.

Lon privately coaches companies on harnessing innovative thinking and social media strategies to create higher productivity and profits. Lon's presentations are personalized to help corporate, government, higher-ed, and non-profit executives improve their operations and performance by capturing their innovative potential. As Lon says, "When you see your world with a different perspective, you see new ways to do everything!"

Contact Lon at: LonSafko@LonSafko.com.

Back to Introduction

Biographies

Dave Kerpen

Dave Kerpen is the founder and CEO of Likeable Local, the cofounder and Chairman of Likeable Media, the NY Times Bestselling author of 3 books, an international keynote speaker, and the #1 LinkedIn Influencer of all time in page views, ahead of Bill Gates, Jack Welch, Mark Cuban, and President Barack Obama.

Likeable Local, a social media software product for small businesses and Likeable Media is an award-winning social media and word-of-mouth marketing firm with triple digit revenue growth for 4 consecutive years. Likeable Media was named to both the 2011 and 2012 Inc. 500 list of fastest growing private companies in the United States. In 2012 and 2013, Likeable Media was named one of Crain's Best Places to Work in NYC.

Following a sponsored wedding which raised over $100,000 including $20K for charity, Dave and his wife Carrie started and transformed the KBuzz (founded in 2007) into Likeable Media, one of Facebook's Top 65 Preferred Developer Consultants as well as the only 3-time WOMMY Award winner for excellence from the Word of Mouth Marketing Association (WOMMA) and one of the 500 fastest growing private companies in the US according to INC Magazine for both 2011 and 2012.

Dave blogs twice a week on LinkedIn as part of LinkedIn's Thought Leader Program and is the 25th most followed person in the world, with more than 300,000 followers, which is growing at about 3000 followers a week. In 2013, Dave's blogs received over 16 million total page views, including the most popular article of all time, *11 Simple Concepts To Become a Better Leader*", with 2.5 million page views, ahead of Bill Gates, Tony

Robbins, Barack Obama, Jack Welch, Ariana Huffington, and Richard Branson.

Dave has been featured on CNBC's "On the Money", BBC, ABC World News Tonight, the CBS Early Show, the New York Times, and countless blogs. Dave has also keynoted at dozens of conferences across the globe and webinars for organizations such as WOMMA, TEDx, SXSW, and the American Marketing Association.

Dave reaches an additional 100K followers through social media, his subscriber list, and is backed by a team of 75 social media thought leaders who collectively have managed over 250 accounts on Facebook and other social networks for Verizon, 1-800 Flowers.com, Neutrogena, Logitech, Pampered Chef, G.E, Medtronic, Restaurant.com, & Heineken.

Dave's 1st book was a NY Times bestseller – Likeable Social Media: How to Delight Your Customers, Create an Irresistible Brand, and Be Generally Amazing on Facebook and other social networks. His 2nd book, Likeable Business: Why Today's Consumers Demand More and How Leaders Can Deliver, debuted November 2, 2012.

Contact Dave at: Dave@Likeable.com

Made in the USA
San Bernardino, CA
09 April 2017